# THE YEAR OF
# NO MONEY
# IN TOKYO

# THE YEAR OF NO MONEY IN TOKYO

## WAYNE LIONEL APONTE

WATKINS
& McKAY

Wilmington 2009

Copyright © 2009 by Wayne Lionel Aponte

All rights reserved.
Printed in the United States of America.
First edition

This book, or parts thereof, may not be reproduced in any form
without the prior permission of Watkins & McKay, LLC.

For information about permission to reproduce selections from this
book, write to Watkins & McKay, LLC
PMB 6595, 2711 Centerville Road, Suite 120
Wilmington, DE 19808

Portions of this book were published in *The Washington Post*.

Publisher's Cataloging-In-Publication Data
(Prepared by The Donohue Group, Inc.)

Aponte, Wayne Lionel.
The year of no money in Tokyo / Wayne Lionel Aponte.—1st ed.

p. cm.

Issued also in audio format.
ISBN: 978-0-9820550-0-7 (hardcover)
ISBN: 978-0-9820550-1-4 (pbk.)

1. Aponte, Wayne Lionel--Travel. 2. Aliens--Japan--Tokyo--Biography.
3. Americans--Japan--Biography. 4. Japan--Social life and customs--20th
century. 5. Japan--Description and travel. I. Title.

DS832.7.A6 A65 2009

952.049/092

For Christine Aponte

**Acknowledgments**
Many thanks to: Marie Brown, Faith Childs,
Sarah Cypher, John Deiner, Michael Dyer,
Henry Finder, Henry Louis Gates, Jr.,
Karen Reddick, and Laurie Viera Rigler.

*Be a man where you are... and force your way to intelligence, wealth, and respectability. If you can't do that here; you can't do that there.*

Frederick Douglass, 1852

*While the tale of how we suffer, and how we are delighted, and how we may triumph is never new, it always must be heard. There isn't any other to tell, it's the only light we've got in all this darkness... And this tale, according to that face, that body, those strong hands on those strings, has another aspect in every country, and a new depth in every generation.*

James Baldwin, *The Price of the Ticket*

*The fiction I write is intensely personal. There's a lot of isolation, there's a lot of thwarted ambition, there's a lot of obstacles which have to be surmounted, there's a lot about class. I could put in all sorts of signifiers about loneliness, or about worry, or about hope, but a lot of commentators would look at it and think, well it's about race.*

Caryl Phillips, Distance learner, *The Observer*, 23 March 2003

**A Note About The Author**

Wayne Lionel Aponte lives and works in Tokyo, Japan. His writing has appeared in *The New York Times*, *The Washington Post*, *The Wall Street Journal*, *The Financial Times* (London), and *The Nation*.

# Contents

CHAPTER ONE

## A Space Between Nightmares

SOUNDS OF CHILDREN'S LAUGHTER, then a motorcycle's acceleration, the metal clap of the outside mailbox, and the doorbell of the adjacent home. A young woman shouts a greeting in the upper range of her soprano voice. A door slams shut. A bird chirps. Someone coughs. A helicopter sends its thudding vibrations into the wooden-framed window of my three-tatami-mat room. So much for sleep. So much for tranquility.

There are white walls trimmed in brown panels. A large map of Southeast Asia decorates one. On the other, a small closet holds several boxes. Coats, towels, shirts, and suits hang on a white plastic rod that spans the width of the space.

The room's only window offers no sunlight, even on the brightest of days. The view is underwhelming: a metal gate, beyond which are a few simple concrete houses, separated by an arm's distance. I live in a coffin. Although I'm average height, I can touch its wooden ceiling without lifting my heels. From the center of the floor, I can place my fingertips against both walls at the same time.

I used to share a six-tatami-mat room in a different Tokyo guesthouse with a voluptuous twenty-one-year-old hostess. She was Irish, and nice, and she didn't mind having a male room-mate. During our three weeks together, I learned a lot from her.

She often returned late, dressed extravagantly, only to doze off in her clothes. The next morning, her ritual included a walk to the bathroom to rid her face of its smeared makeup. Then, she changed her clothes on her side of the room and departed before eight for what seemed an unending search for day work. Overall, she must have felt very comfortable around me. She never emp-tied the trash. She usually left socks and blouses on the floor. So much for pride. So much for cleanliness. So much for self-love.

We didn't talk much. She came to Tokyo to earn money for her studies in Ireland. She was totally preoccupied with money; how to get it, and how to associate herself with those who have it—just like me.

"A Japanese man offered me $5,000 to sleep with him," she said one early morning. If only he could see her unmasked. Questions about her experience produced hysterical laughter. She claimed to reject his offer.

When she moved out, I asked the landlords if I might rent the entire room, but they had already promised the other half to a new tenant. And, without having to say so, they made it clear that two tenants earned them more money.

"Don't worry," he said, head tilted, teeth exposed, "she's Japanese."

I was supposed to respond: "Oh, yes, of course." As the Chi-nese saying goes, a man's most coveted possessions are an Ameri-can house, Chinese food, a European car, and a Japanese wife. To possess those things is to live.

He played to the stereotype of the fastidious maternal

Japanese woman. And I believed him. The more I thought about the chance to improve my knowledge of contemporary Japanese culture and language, free of charge, the more I liked the idea. What I liked even more was the possibility of—how shall I say—connecting in a more physical way with a native woman. I have always wondered about how Japanese and American women differ in private.

Yet, on the day she moved in, I assumed that she had run away from home. She managed to squeeze into the small room: a huge glass cabinet filled with shoes, books, papers, cups, and other memorabilia; a worn gray sofa, a moderately sized table with an oval-shaped mirror attached, and a long rack of clothes that couldn't fit inside the closet beside my things.

Additionally, she decorated the walls with her own art—a spider's web made out of wire, and silk-screened reproductions of a male friend, placing his hand inside her blouse.

For a single occupant, the room, with all her objects, was crowded. For two people, the place was a fire hazard. To accommodate her belongings, she pushed my things to the side. So much for first impressions. So much for common courtesy. So much for communication.

Her name was Mamiko. I wanted to throw her out, but the situation appeared beyond my control. At first she had her own large room on the ground floor, until the landlords moved her in with me, and put another woman into her former room.

The perils of living in a Tokyo guesthouse.

Against this backdrop, I received an ultimatum to "work it out or move out." Without much choice, I forced myself to adjust. I vowed to stay long enough to save money for my own place.

2

One evening, Mamiko locked the door from the inside.

"Chotto matte kudasai," she said. *Wait just a minute, please.* The door squeaked open. In the dim light, I eyed a woman, head bowed, dressed in a loose robe. Over her shoulder, a white male peeked out from the sheets of her sofa bed. Had any mention of possible guests entered our brief chats? Had a message appeared on my desk? Can't he take you to a hotel? He doesn't have his own room? We share this room, you know; this isn't your own place. What if you take a shower, while he's here, and suddenly something of mine disappears?

The mysterious man eventually put on his pants and departed. His was the first but not last face I would see in her covers. Mamiko's selfishness foreshadowed other later events, too. Unemployed, she slept until the afternoon, and went to sleep in the early morning hours. In between that time, while I worked, she frolicked with some of the other thirteen members of the guesthouse, inside our room or in the kitchen.

As one obsessed with privacy, I dreaded the possibility of someone rifling through my belongings in my absence. I never invited anyone home as a rule, because I carried a profound sense of shame about my living arrangements—my roommate in particular. Often I came home to find scraps of rubbish in the middle of the floor she had dragged home in hopes of turning it into art. When she worked late on these projects, she did so to loud pop music. She dreamt of becoming a professional artist and holding an exhibition in Tokyo. "Sex," she said, "boosted her creative energy."

I have no idea how Mamiko funded her life. Perhaps her

family helped. Despite the abundant amount of time on her hands, she outperformed the previous roommate in terms of untidiness: abandoned bowls of rice or cereal, splayed-open fashion magazines, CDs, cigarette butts, pink socks turned inside out, a bag from Dunkin' Donuts, a pair of purple suede platform shoes, and even blood-stained panties. So much for the Western image of Japanese women. My former roommate had shortcomings, but her work took her out of the flat in the evenings, so at the very least, I could count on regular blocks of solitude. With Mamiko, there was no such luxury.

Late at night, I awakened to the sound of heavy breathing, and sporadic whispers of "Sugoi," *great.* A look behind the long rack full of clothes revealed Mamiko, nude and masturbating. Under different circumstances, I might have joined her. But my desire was dulled by the fear of others finding out and the nearness of other rooms, and more than anything, the sight annoyed me.

The day she tried to steal one of my ties, my patience left me. But the landlord brushed off my request for a replacement, saying only to work it out with her myself. English words alone were useless. Another Japanese woman lived in the house, and I asked her if she might intervene using her mother tongue. But she explained that Mamiko came from a "bad family," and must have thought any intervention at all was useless. She would not help.

A few weeks later, I returned from work to a room thick with marijuana smoke. Eyes red, smirk on her round face, Mamiko claimed innocence. But the smell, coupled with evidence in the ashtray, and later in her glass cabinet, suggested otherwise. I admit, I wanted this kind of excuse. What you do in your free time is your own business. But in a living situation like ours, there are consequences even then. If a neighbor complained to the Japanese police, the police would identify the odor's exact location, find me here, and conclude that the foreigner uses and perhaps sells drugs, just like in those Hollywood movies. He's contaminating the Japanese race, they'd say. Police were not known for their clemency.

All guesthouse residents, upon moving in, signed an acknowledgment that drug possession will result in swift eviction. No questions asked. I informed management, invited them to the room, showed them evidence, and nothing happened. Not only did she remain, but she smoked weed in the room again.

It became clear. If you are Japanese in Japan, you get one free crime, especially when the object of that crime is a foreigner. A few weeks later, I moved out.

And that is how I ended up in this oversized coffin. It was all I could afford. Yet the evening I moved in, my new home felt as lavish as a penthouse. Privacy! I slid shut the wooden door. Then I baptized the three-tatami-mat room with a wild, uninhibited, violent dance to a syncopated drumbeat, sanctified with a thick bass line. I was so happy—and so relieved. It didn't matter that my room was adjacent to a toilet and that through the thin walls I could hear my neighbors and their functions. Nor did it matter that the room was closest to the public telephone, which rang at all hours of the night. Didn't even matter that here three people was a crowd. Nothing meant more than privacy.

Mine was one of seven rooms within a traditional, two-floor home, converted into a gaijin house—the locals' term for these places meant for foreigners. They attract mostly short-term visitors. I spoke with the other occupants only when I could not avoid it. Meeting them was like trying to remove a particle from my eye with an index finger. I still had the rawness of entering a new atmosphere for the first time. Encounters necessitated that

I explain myself, my work, my life. I was insecure. I preferred to be in my room, away from people and gossip. There was no need to speak; one could gather information from eavesdropping. My neighbors worked as hostesses, English teachers, or bar employees, and hailed from America, England, Australia, and Israel.

Months later, I quit my job as a seller of English-language courses to Japanese university students. The bureaucracy, politics, and sheer burden of persuading them, and their parents, in Japanese, to part with $6,000, during a recession—together it was enough to make one turn psychotic. However, the experience improved my Japanese significantly and I had made a few sales. Still, the gains failed to offset the demands: Monday to Saturday, nine to nine, three hundred daily calls to attract students to the sales pitch. Most of them cancelled their appointments at the last minute. At the end of each week, my left eardrum hummed.

I figured that finding newer, higher-paying, and less-stressful Tokyo work would be easy. Thought that I was immune to unemployment, despite the slowing Japanese economy. With my credentials and enough savings to last a couple of months, I told myself I was bound to land something.

Day by day, week by week, and month by month, I searched. Found myself counting time by Mondays, the day one of the newspapers posted job listings. Three more Mondays till the end of the month, I would think. I checked boards in the Foreign Correspondents' Club of Japan and in supermarkets that sold imported products. Made random calls to companies in the phone book, sector by sector. And day by day the interviews appeared sporadically, week by week the rejection letters increased, and month by month I became less hopeful and more humiliated.

During my low moments, I sought positions as an English teacher. They cited my lack of teaching experience. I applied for a waiter's job. When the restaurants rejected my application, my last interview was a secret one for a dishwasher's post at a Japanese restaurant.

"We only hire foreigners married to natives," said the manager.

That's when the walls started caving in. That's when this room began resembling death. The syncopated beats and thick bass lines to which I once danced alone changed to the slower, elongated, legato tones of an American's requiem. The sounds of people attending to their natural functions in the nearby bathroom disgusted me. News reports about the yen's steady appreciation against the US dollar, to a historic postwar high of 79, only mocked my poverty.

The helicopter passes over the roof again. The girl yells another soprano greeting. Yearning for companionship, I lift myself from the futon, step to my desk, turn on the computer, and for the first time in a while, started typing.

I have no job prospects. I have no idea how to lift myself from the edge of the underclass, from the edge of starvation in Tokyo, umpteen miles away from my home in New York City. So, I shall dedicate the early morning hours to telling the story of this period of my life in Japan—to pass the time, to keep from going insane in the year of the wild boar, the year of no money.

CHAPTER TWO

## Shedding Pretensions

THE CLIMATE IN JAPAN is one of caution, skepticism, and unhappiness. The 1980s were an economic bacchanal, and the '90s were a sort of Ramadan, the Muslim period of fasting. Japan's gross national product is down. The high yen threatens to choke profits at already hurting exporters. The Japanese stock market hits abysmal new lows. The nation once regarded on the verge of becoming an economic superpower now drags through a recession, which experts expect to worsen considerably before improving slightly. What happened? How did Japan manage to squander its success?

According to Richard Katz, in *Japan: The System That Soured*, the country lost track of its purpose. In the 1950s and '60s, Katz writes that Japan nurtured and protected young industries in an effort to eventually compete with the West. Businesses in sectors from car making to electronics all had the potential to gain global profit shares. At the same time, Katz argues that Japan aided industries with no chance of becoming exporters, such as aviation and chemicals.

As the local economy matured, in the 1970s, the nation's approach started hurting long-term economic progress. But that didn't stop Japan from protecting the unprofitable and promoting the profitable. Thus, the process created a dual economy of world-class exporters and remarkably weak—but politically connected—domestic sectors.

Consumers around the world marveled at Sony electronic gadgets. They spent hard-earned money on automobiles produced by Toyota, Nissan, Honda, and Mazda. (For years, Honda cars were one of the top-selling vehicles in the United States.) Inside Japan, however, far from eyes unable to decipher Japanese kanji characters, the story was altogether a different one. The manufacturing sectors, such as food processing and textiles, were protected from competition and got lazy by international standards. According to Katz, they failed to ever become competitive. The stronger domestic exporters picked up the slack by supporting the weaker sectors, until they decided to invest in markets abroad, in the name of sanity and profitability. In turn, Japan simply compensated for inefficiencies by investing heavily in losing sectors.

Meanwhile, the strong Japanese stock market enabled borrowers to repay lenders with their own shares, rather than in cash, by using convertible bonds—that is, a bond that the holder can convert to a set number of common shares. With that money, companies expanded operations internationally, established more jobs and made further inroads into overseas markets.

But the crash of the Japanese stock market forced Japanese companies to repay all of their loans in cash, not stocks, a Herculean task, since the plunge in share prices wiped out hundreds of billions of dollars in a day. The result hit companies first, which were burdened with gargantuan debt, as well as the banks—many of which would go bankrupt, and others were forced to merge. The damage spread outward to the rest of the economy.

The swagger is gone from both the nation and the individual. Some elite bureaucrats are beginning to speak out about the need for aggressive reform and are reexamining long-held myths about Japan. Sakura Shiga, a former director of the Economic Planning Agency's Planning division, doesn't mince words while pointedly addressing the issues.

> All of our long-cherished assumptions—that the Japanese economy will always grow, that asset prices will always rise, that full employment is virtually guaranteed, that financial institutions are invulnerable, that Japan has the safest society in the world—are now overturned.
>
> People in Japan are losing self-confidence and wondering what has gone wrong. In short, we are aware that we are in a crisis for the first time in these fifty years of post-war prosperity, and we know we have to revamp our society and economy.

The barrage of downbeat news changed the Japanese attitude toward the Western Other. People need scapegoats, a place to direct their bottled-up frustration. Hostility and aggression have been increasing overall, and in varying degrees, against foreign presences here. A small number of profitable Western-based brokerages received bomb threats by fax. By using business techniques honed in their home countries, they have been able to stay in the black despite Japan's sinking stock market; furthermore, with many computer-driven programs, there is no need for Japanese-speaking staff or Japanese customers. I interviewed a vice president of a now-bankrupt domestic securities firm years ago, and he thought that success by non-Japanese companies, amid recession, persuades the envious to regard them as undeservedly lucky. "Every government," he said, "protects their own people against foreign people."

His talk might be a microcosm of what ordinary Japanese think. I get the impression that locals believe they can treat me however they want, without repercussions. I have inherited the anger, panic, and pain of these Tokyo times. I feel the environment hardening me, gradually gnawing away at my will to survive, my humanity, like termites slowly devouring the foundation of a wooden home. I become irritable by the slightest things. I struggle to maintain my sanity.


2


What does all of this mean for common people? For Japanese housewives on their way to the supermarket for some radish and strips of beef, bad business conditions mean cutting back on consumption. For local professionals, the possibility of losing a job, something unthinkable during the good times. For university students scheduled to soon enter the workforce, it means limited, if any, full-time job prospects.

Recession separates the strong from the weak, the prepared from the unprepared, the skilled from the unskilled. Only in a remarkably desperate period of Japanese history can a book such as Wataru Tsurumi's *The Complete Manual of Suicide* consistently appear on local bestseller lists. Since its publication in 1993, over a million copies have been sold, in tandem with the nation's increasing suicide rate. Tsurumi wants readers to know that whenever they get bored with life, the choice to kill themselves exists. The book provides instructions for ten suicide methods, including electrocution, self-immolation, hanging, overdosing on drugs, freezing, and jumping off buildings and in front of express trains.

"When you have no bank account," or hardly any money in one, "no car, no health insurance, it inverts the slogan of that best-selling self-help book: you have to sweat the small stuff," wrote Ron Suskind, in a *New York Times* book review of David K. Shipler's *The Working Poor: Invisible in America*. It becomes one of my mantras.

I walk down the street and people blow cigarette smoke toward my face or flick ashes near my clothes, or they raise and extend their elbows close to my head. I order food at a restaurant; as I raise the soup spoon toward my mouth, I see four staff members staring at me grinning. I put down the spoon and motion to take a sip of iced tea and their eyes bulge. I neither eat, nor drink, nor pay the bill.

I skim a biography and another customer on the foreign-books floor accuses me of theft, because I won't allow him to look over my shoulder for a read with me. He's an aristocratically dressed, older Japanese. "Let me see. Let me see," he squeaks. His soy-sauce breath attacks my nostrils. I look again at the cover of the book to assure myself that I haven't been reading pornography—it's a biography about F. Scott Fitzgerald. "You must be trying to steal it," he adds. He repeats his strange logic to the shop's staff, who have been eyeing my every move from the outset.

I go to Yokohama museum to see Robert Frank's collection of one hundred and sixty photographs titled "Moving Out." Next, I stop by Yurindo bookstore in Landmark Tower. While reading through a collection of essays, I hear a click and see a flash. An adjacent Japanese couple has just taken my picture. For them, seeing me with a book is like seeing a seal balance a ball on its nose or a dolphin leap out of the water for a meal. I feel robbed and want to retaliate by taking the camera, opening the back, and exposing the film. These days, my anger is quick to rise. If only stares could assault. Sushi-eating motherfuckers. The next person with the audacity to do that will experience permanent damage, I tell myself.

Meanwhile, job interviews are even more confrontational. I prepare myself like an athlete before a race. I do calisthenics, research the company, and play speed chess against a small machine for mental agility. Yet I don't know fully the content and direction of the interviewer's thoughts. I try to match my experiences and skills with the responsibilities of the positions on offer. They, on the other hand, focus on something different.

"Do you have a girlfriend?" asks the local firm's native representative.

"I beg your pardon."

"Do you have a girlfriend?"

"Do I need a girlfriend to proofread documents here?"

"Just answer the question. DO YOU HAVE A GIRLFRIEND?"

I sense agitation in his voice. I feel my temperature rising and muscles tightening.        "Yes, I do."

"Is she Japanese?"

"What does that have to do with this position?"

"Answer the question."

"That's none of your business."

The company sends the rejection letter on the same day.

On other occasions, interviewers fire rapid questions at me, interrogation-style. Or they tell me over the phone that Japanese isn't necessary for the position available, but once I enter the office, they ask me detailed questions about my foreign-language ability, and interview me in Japanese for an English-language editorial job.

I operate from a position of economic weakness and society wants to keep it that way. I can't negotiate. I think potential employers know that I struggle financially. If I turn down an offer, which I haven't had the luxury to do, or if I ask for more money, I feel that they'll yank the carpet from under my feet. I need enough money in my account to decline unfavorable offers and to stand up for myself with a clear conscious. In other words, I need fuck-you money.

3

An air of carnival transforms Tokyo's Omotesando Street on the second day of the new year. Shoulder to shoulder, hordes of people ease along the sidewalks in measured steps: couples young and old, families and children, hand in hand. Kimono-clad women distinguish themselves in my consciousness for the first time. My admiration grows steadily, and I ask a few of them to pose in a photograph with me. They all oblige without hesitation.

Several booths form a chain along the tree-lined street closest to Harajuku Station. Each advertises its specialties in large Japanese characters on flapping, bright-colored cloth: yaki-soba (thin, fried noodles in soy sauce), oden (mixed vegetables), and takoyaki (octopus dumplings). Two men set up stands that boast pastel portraits of Marilyn Monroe and Sylvester Stallone. They offer to draw your picture for 1,500 yen, or about fifteen dollars. The site of such creations offsets the newcomer's expectations for drawings of Asian faces.

A solitary man gives massages. The back wall of his space is bedecked with photocopied articles about him and his training schools, and people watch his demonstration on an older

Japanese woman's shoulders. In tandem with each squeeze, she says how good it feels.

In the street, a crowd surrounds a clown. While balancing on a unicycle, he juggles three bowling pins, three pieces of wood set afire, and five metal rings. In acts of careful theatrical management, he skillfully catches several behind his back and through his legs. During breaks, he works the crowd with simple games of call and response in broken Japanese. They enjoy his foreign accent. They like him so much they place money into his hat when the show ends.

As I cross below the overpass leading to Yoyogi Park, I see a man with an olive complexion, dressed in a yellow sweatshirt and black pants. He stands before a metal chain that blocks off the street. He sports a long Santa Claus hat. Right arm extended, elbow slightly bent, he holds out a red tin cup. When one Japanese family walks by, he motions to a small boy of about seven. The boy passes; the man frowns. I observed a similar scene in San Francisco on the piers of Fisherman's Wharf. I assume that the man would have begun dancing the moment the coins hit the bottom of his cup, and the amount of money would probably dictate the length and the complexity of his performance. But the more I study that man, pondering whether or not to take his photograph, the more ashamed I become. I am ashamed of, and troubled over, him. He reminds me of myself. Will I be wearing a Santa Claus hat this time next year? The truth of the matter is that I can't dance.

Hoping not to make eye contact, hoping not to distract him, I rush passed, staring straight ahead. Several feet away, I turn around. His cup is at his side, and his eyes fix on mine.

## 4

Four more women in red kimonos inch toward the overpass. I persuade someone to take a photograph of me between two of the heavily made-up women. The stranger fancies herself an expert; a shot from a distance may be better than a close-up, she says. It would capture the full length of the kimono. I hold my tongue and allow her to use my camera to take one closer and another farther away. How pleasing to support my Tokyo memories with photographs.

All Japanese women look beautiful in traditional garb. I follow their backs, and they vanish gradually into the crowds of dark blue and black overcoats. It is at this moment that I hear a rattle of a drum.

Looking down from the overpass, I see a huge crowd of people gathering in the middle of the street. Straining my neck for a better view, I eye three casually dressed black men alongside a Japanese man. One plays the drums in short spurts. The others take in the crowd, which now expands into a huge force. Suddenly, the drummer extends a rapid rhythm and out jumps one of the black males. He glides, as best as he can, on the street's tar and gravel surface. His performance generates a chorus of shouts. So many Japanese people convene that, from a distance, one might think a famous singer decided to give a free public concert. At once I infer, from the extraordinary interest, how foreigners are perceived here.

Before the dancers can get any money from the large crowd, a police car interrupts them. Over the loudspeaker, an officer speaks slowly in Japanese: "I don't speak English, but the streets are too crowded for the cars to pass." He adds, "The streets are not made for dancing." The crowd laughs. The Japanese member of the dance group provides a translation to the rest of the troupe, but diplomatically excludes the part meant to insult them.

The first week of the New Year is the loneliest time for those people without friends and money. The holiday could not have come at a worse time. The city streets empty, as natives spend time with family. Most businesses close. I shop for groceries at convenience stores or eat at fast food restaurants. On December 31, droves of Japanese people make their visit to Meiji Jingu Shrine, where they pray for a better year. I do, too, but from my room. A private ceremony mostly in my head. Please, please, please. Just one more Tokyo job and I'll stop with the women, the spending, and the shirking of dedicated Japanese-language study.

Why endure such dire straits, I wonder. Well, I haven't got a choice. When times get rough, others have their family's wealth, their father's company, some equity, credit cards, or connections to fall back on. I have absolutely nothing.

Going home to America, of course, might help. Some kind of work would turn up. At the very least, I wouldn't worry about a place to stay. But returning home poorer than when I left, or even mentioning my condition on the phone, would look like defeat. It would be an utter embarrassment. A person must maintain his sense of self, such as it is; and for me, portraying my time abroad as a professional success story was important.

Besides, I have something to prove. I can survive. I will bulldoze my way to financial security. My success will defy those forces that desire my suffering—so I hope.

5

Not too long ago, I lived in a place big enough for a Japanese family, in an expensive district. The apartment was luxurious by Japanese standards: a couple of rooms in a nice building, a bike ride away from the office. My Japanese colleagues all lived an hour away in company dormitories.

We hang so much on the most superficial of hooks. We so often perceive our *self* in relation to external circumstances: a job with a prestigious company, a home full of luxury goods at a choice address. I hung my life on those hooks. I figured that if I lived in an exclusive area, and worked at a reputable firm, people would like and respect me.

It didn't matter whether I liked doing the job. The questions facing me then weren't how to pay next month's rent or what to eat, as they are now. Instead, as a wire-service reporter, I wondered about the direction of the Japanese government bond market. The pressure to produce and to beat the competition was substantial. Management favored speed, accuracy, and prolific output. The writing demands of a daily newspaper are more relaxed: two articles a week would earn colleagues' respect. At the information service, however, one met expectations by writing five to seven articles a day. Imagine the amount of time required to fulfill the responsibility.

Youth, money, and a plush apartment, in the center of Tokyo, is a dangerous combination. It was a period of work and wealth, but also one of remarkable waste. Rather than spending my leisure on exercise and hobbies, saving money and learning the language, I squandered energy, money, and my midtwenties on perfumed Japanese fantasies.

It's fair to say it was my hobby—a costly one. Addicted to hearing women shriek high-pitched praises in bed. Embracing whole that figment of the Asian imagination about the Western male's sensuality. Although others have lived a lifestyle similar to mine, a failure to learn from their experiences is precisely why poverty and his cousins, humiliation and doubt, have sought out my company repeatedly, persistently—and successfully.

## 6

Had I not lost my job, I would probably still consider materialism a byword for prosperity. Unemployment is a good teacher. Not only did it teach me that I couldn't work amid the politics of a competitive corporation, it stressed that my priorities at the time only attracted distress and resentment.

Potential Japanese employers looked unfavorably upon my address. They thought that I would demand too high a salary. They resented me for living extravagantly, with good reason: the nation was in the middle of its worst recession since WWII. The close-knit community of business journalists made it difficult to find lucrative, full-time work; they regarded me as damaged goods, since I hadn't made it past the trial period of my old job. No help, either, were the enemies out to destroy my reputation. Unable to justify living in an expensive apartment without a steady income, I had no choice but to move into a gaijin house.

The problem with hanging one's ideas of success on superficial hooks is that when those hooks fail—when the address changes, when the income falters—the feeling of defeat is total. My dwindling savings are far from a safety net. They are more like a tightrope. My life is unusually solitary and frugal, and my entertainment is limited to reading, writing, and watching television rather than socializing at restaurants, bars, and night-clubs. Yet, I try to operate without panic on the hopes that my situation will improve.

When I entered the chambers of poverty, I went through a series of transformations. The first stage brought feelings of self-consciousness and shame. The second; anger and bitterness. The third; numbness toward my squalor. I was beyond caring. The fourth stage introduced a comfort within my humble situation, and I made the most of it.

Through each phase, as I gently descended into the abyss, I de-veloped a fidelity to the art of interpretation. In other words, I re-invented myself. In the beginning, I avoided people because they inevitably wanted to learn about my profession and employer. I hated talking about my condition. I was too proud to say, "I'm unemployed and am close to being homeless. Would you happen to know of any work?"

By chance, I encountered a woman acquaintance, an Ameri-can, in a Tokyo music shop. I met her at the height of my arrogant period, and before we even have hello out of the way, she starts with the ridicule. She says that she called my former employer a while ago only to learn that I no longer worked there.

"So, how many jobs have you had?" she asks.

So much for pleasantries. So much for suitable small talk. So much for keeping the harmony. She's bent on issuing petty insults. She waxes philosophic about American men who mis-represent themselves at U.S. parties to impress the women. The implication is that I am that type of man. I want to say that I'm the one who is still out here fighting the economic battle. I'm the courageous one. I haven't given up. I'm not in the class of men who avoid work. But I interrupt her monologue and say how good it is to see her again, and walk away.

Japanese women protect the pride of their men in public. I observed a woman slip her partner some money as they neared the cashier of a sandwich shop, to spare him the embarrassment of an empty wallet. Capitalist societies are so dedicated to success—actual and the appearance of—that failure is taboo. Losing one's job is a kind of personal shame worn inside. So, during the unavoidable encounters with old acquaintances, or initiated meetings with new ones, I started telling people that I'm writing books. I said it so often that I persuaded that the intelligible lie on the surface, to paraphrase Milan Kundera, was the unintelligible truth underneath: I now had an occupation and the time to sit, read, and think. I converted my struggles into art. I looked at written ideas, contemplated ways to present material, conducted research, and transcribed text to computer disk. The process sustains and distracts me.

It doesn't, however, feed me or keep me company or pay.

7

A few weeks into 1995, my bad luck holds. Then, encouragement comes from an unlikely source. A natural disaster.

The Kobe earthquake claims thousands of Japanese lives and leaves just as many homeless. Japan is shocked. On the news, Prime Minister Tomiichi Murayama tells victims to keep strong and work hard—how detached and unsympathetic are his statements. Scenes of survivors. Homes of rubble.

My suffering is selfish and insignificant. If I had time only to remove one thing from the house, what would I take? Where would I go afterward? Can't even fathom a response. The incident removes a burden from my back and delivers a sense of optimism and renewal. I focus on the narcissistic and wasteful nature of collecting things. I feel so light and so lucky just to be alive and in good health. Life can be a lot worse. I'm grateful for the basics: a cramped room, food to eat, and a couple of coins to last another week or so.

As I near the end of my funds, I receive a box of old mail from New York. Sorting through the bills, bills, and more bills, I open a financial statement. It states that I have some money in a U.S. bank account I hadn't used in about three years. How could I have forgotten? It's only a little over a thousand dollars, but that's enough to buy more time. I make arrangements for a money transfer, pay my rent, and return for another round of job hunting.

# CHAPTER THREE

## Reciprocity

MONEY HAD ALWAYS BEEN my bulwark against romantic distractions in Tokyo. If I had money, I was in charge of the itinerary. I arranged meetings at my convenience—usually at night, two or three times a month. We rarely went to my apartment. It took less of my time that way.

Joblessness changes everything. Now, I feel compelled to meet women whenever possible, listen intensely, and shower them with attention and affection. Otherwise, I am too proud to accept their help. Dependency makes me feel like a whore.

During my first months of poverty, I moved in with a woman in an effort to cut my cash-burn rate. Living together made her happy because it prevented me from visiting other women. I was her possession, and lived under a tacit house arrest.

Well, that lasted for a few weeks. As I left one morning for an important job interview, she told me I would find my belongings in the corridor when I returned, and that she had made arrangements to have the locks changed. She accused me of cheating on her. She wanted to teach me a lesson. Fortunately, I had another woman who was adamant enough in her devotion to rescue me from such a fate. With her help,

I moved into a guesthouse the very next day and paid two months' rent in advance.

I approached other women I dated when I was wealthy. They had received free gifts, meals, and entertainment. I didn't believe I would ever need to cash in, but in my poverty, in matters of survival, one does not have the luxury to make decisions that are at once logical, ethical, politically correct, considerate, and proper. Four women remain true. They each offer separate mixtures of love, food, and money. They believe that my stock has bottomed and they want to benefit from a steady rise in its value. Yet, I am less confident. I learn that I must make them feel happy about their generosity, and each meeting is another performance.

The choice between homelessness and using people for access to their homes and food is a matter of survival. I do what is necessary to live better, without compromising my principles completely. If that means relying on others, so be it.

2

I don't exactly hate cats; they bore me. As a topic of discussion during a meal, I endure an extended chat about Nozomi's sister's cat in order to keep a polite atmosphere. Her sister named it Michelangelo. He's cute—and tiny. She centers her life around it, according to Nozomi, because she hasn't had a boyfriend for a very long time. They do practically everything together. They exercise together, sleep together, eat together, watch TV together, and they sometimes even travel together. When she visits her parents in northern Japan, she takes the cat with her.

One day she had run out of cat food and gave it shrimp instead. Why did she do that? Thereafter, the cat refused to eat anything else but shrimp, which cost three times as much as regular cat food in Tokyo. But she couldn't refuse because she has come to love the cat so much … on and on. Nozomi talks for about an hour. With a strained show of enthusiasm, I listen.

Nozomi is the daughter of a post office worker. She left Aomori to study in Tokyo, and worked two years in a hospital as a medical technician, then one year as a fashion coordinator, and now as an insurance salesperson. She's twenty-nine, lonely, yellow-complexioned, well proportioned, with a top set of mostly false, eggshell colored teeth. She has fine, cropped, jet-black hair, penetrating eyes, and smooth skin.

We first met outside of a theater, after seeing an independent French film. We happened to be using the same train line—I, to visit a woman, she, to go home. We talked about the film, the train, and Tokyo, and when we parted we exchanged numbers and kissed on the cheek goodnight. Sex entered the relationship soon afterward and has maintained it since. That's all we did regularly, and we've grown to depend on each other emotionally.

It wasn't until I experienced a reversal of fortune that I spent more time with her and have gotten to know her better. Of all the women I've dated in Tokyo, she's the most independent and most charitable. I identify her by those qualities more than by her beauty. She's also the most vindictive. She's the one who put me out of her apartment. She assumed that I had no place else to go, and after I refused to return on my hands and knees, begging for mercy, she tried to get me back. But it was too late. I had already adjusted to a transient way of life, one without so much trust.

That did not stop me from contacting her out of carnal need a few months later. Although she does not know exactly where I am staying, or with whom, she still campaigns for my full commitment to her. Were it not for the vindictive streak, we would have been married by now.

There are scratch marks on her right hand from the cat. She is wearing a one-piece black Armani dress that brings back memories. She once said she would only wear that dress for an opera in New York City or Tokyo. But given the slim chance of that happening, she wears it tonight to our candlelit dinner in the Ebisu district, at a French restaurant, for which she willingly pays.

Nozomi hands me a box of Neuhaus chocolate for Valentine's Day and a present. According to Japanese custom, women give gifts to men in February, and men return the favor in March, on White Day. It's the book I wanted, *The Japanese Chronicles*, by Nicholas Bouvier. In it, the Swiss travel writer provides numerous historical and personal vignettes about his adventures with poor and humble Japanese people, at a time when he had no money. Maybe his book will inspire my own writing.

3

Then, there's Kumiko. We do a lot of things together on Saturdays, when her husband works.

We first began dating after a compliment about her sterling silver earrings, in the classical music section of Roppongi's Wave. Long after we established a routine, a remarkably happy routine, I asked her how she could justify infidelity. She expressed not a word, tone, or sign of regret, as I had. Her response was frank and blunt: "I don't see him as a husband anymore. He's like my family, my brother. I don't feel the same way I felt when we got married."

Her husband was really married to his company. Two years

ago, work demands had pushed him off the brink, and after a nervous breakdown precipitated by a stressful, workaholic schedule, their relationship began its decline. Kumiko supported him emotionally and financially for two years as he recovered his mental health.

She grew up in hardship. Her father had lived above their means, and as an only child, she felt a strong sense of obligation to support her mother with monthly payments after leaving home. It galled her to do the same for her spouse; it was supposed to be the other way around, wasn't it? She wished to start a family of her own, and the impracticality made her bitter. *He's my husband, but he's getting kind of heavy* became a reverberating slogan. Life wasn't fair. The situation stole her innocence. The man she woke up to has now recovered fully, but in her mind he remains different, and weaker, than the kimono-clad one in their wedding photograph.

On our third date after meeting in Roppongi's Wave, she voiced one of the most memorable and unintended phrases about the state of her marriage. "Finally," she said, on the way to my apartment for the first time, "there's someone to take care of me." And I took care of her that night and on a regular basis until my luck ran out.

Ironically, she often took care of me anyway. When I tried years ago to keep a choice Tokyo apartment I couldn't afford, in a foolish attempt to uphold my meretricious lifestyle, she covered one month's rent.

Today, she wants to take me to see "Natural Born Killers," so she will permit me to increase my debt to her. Watching heavily violent and grotesque movies is right up there with the pleasure I get from putting my hand into a blender set at high. The gratuitous violence ruins my appetite for both food and sex. But she made reservations at a steak restaurant, in Ginza, for a late celebration of Valentine's Day, and I mustn't disappoint.

Of her occupation as a graphic designer I do not wish to write. She makes attempts to sprinkle anecdotes about her job into our conversations—those boring meetings and receptions, those old and new accounts, those company trips—but they bore me so I change the subject when I can.

Like many thirty-something Japanese women, Kumiko has been so busy making and spending money, she's forgotten how to think about anything else. Through me, she's been nurturing an alternative way of living, a dream of sorts, of one day starting a life together in America. I give her no reason to think any different. At the meal's end, she fingers that beautiful black head of hair, from her high chiseled cheekbone to the back of her small, pierced ear. Out of her bag, she hands me a box of Godiva chocolate. Next out is James Campell's *Exile in Paris*. She couldn't find Joe Joseph's *The Japanese: Strange, But Not Strangers*.

Outside, she apologizes for menstruating today and for having to return directly home. She thinks I'm disappointed. She grabs my hand to emphasize her sincerity. She doesn't know how much the film's rape scenes sickened me. I wouldn't have to plead illness; the reprieve was like a chilled, foamy glass of Guinness on a hot, sticky summer's day, filled with marathon games of basketball. Hallelujah.

4

Positive thinking does not work. This month brings a dozen rejection letters and six unsuccessful interviews. I'm surprised the bank hasn't cut our business relationship; it spends more money in correspondence than I have in my account. I have 126 yen in my Japanese savings account. Ten thousand yen to my name. Can't even pay next month's rent. As much as I'm against depending on others, it looks like I'll have to surrender pride, if nothing improves by next week. The leverage of an imminent job would make begging for a short-term loan less painful and less humiliating.

Employed, I used to whine about having no time to enjoy life. Unemployed, I now have too much time and don't do a lot. For the day's meal, I eat two bananas, a half bag of Doritos, and drink a can of Fanta grape soda from a vending machine.

For excitement, I turn on the radio. TLC's "Creep," Mary J. Blige's "Be Happy," Boyz II Men's "I'll Make Love To You" and "On Bended Knee" are played in heavy rotation, as well as Bruce Springsteen's "Philadelphia," Annie Lennox's "No More I Love You's" and Ini Kamoze's "Here Comes The Hotstepper." Based on my ignorance of world news, you'd think I lived in a coma. I crack the window and peek outside at the rain. Turn off the radio and scan a book. Open a box of belongings and reread old love letters.

Lethargic and depressed, I doze off for another eight hours. I've conditioned myself to live this uncivilized life. Usually, this rented space is a place not for sleeping, but for changing clothes, checking mail, and writing cover letters for job applications. Days here are simply the space between nightmares.

I usually avoid it at night because of the frequent visitors to the guesthouse. Even during the days, I use a padlock on the door just to visit the shared bathroom, which is four steps away. When I slide shut the door, I wedge it closed with an umbrella because you can't lock it from the inside. I hadn't always taken such precautions. Last month I had dashed out of the shower for some forgotten toiletries, and found some suspicious people standing outside my then-insecure room. Soon after, while I lay reading, enjoying my solitude, someone slid open my door. I invested in the padlock.

For the other residents and their friends, everyday is Saturday. They can afford to be convivial. On many nights, the police respond to complaints from our neighbors about the parties. I now understand why some Japanese landlords discriminate against foreigners.

5

Where do Yoshie and Ayako fit into this ordeal? Both cultivate my privacy and serve as an escape from the insomniacs.

Yoshie invites me over for dinner twice a week, when her sister works the night shift at a hospital. Ayako lives alone, a ten minutes' walk away. Whenever I spend the night, she leaves me her key in the morning. That courtesy gives me blocks of time to use her phone for work searches, to cook, and to relax in solitude. I leave before her shift finishes and place the key in the mailbox.

For the most part, my excursions with Yoshie are what most young Tokyo couples do on weekends. We stroll hand in hand to Aoyama for a Western-style brunch at Luchan's. The punctual trains take us to Shimbashi, where we swap gossip in Hama Rikyu Garden, and watch people ignore the signs to stay off the grass. We listen to music in CD shops.

In a bookstore, we find our different sections. While I browse the English titles, she goes first to the computer texts out of a sense of professional duty, then ends up among books on dining and cooking. She draws my attention to a series of volumes about restaurants in Japan with good interiors. Throughout, the curiosity of locals brings us amusement and intimacy. That night, she prepares a radish salad, penne and spinach, salmon, rice, broccoli, and miso soup. I'm lucky. Without her love, my meal of the day would have been a brownie bought from 7-Eleven for fifty-six yen.

Her parents show up at the apartment the next afternoon from Shizuoka. They're in town to help the younger brother find a cheap room for his university studies. While they are still in the car, Yoshie gives me some pocket money—no questions asked, no strings attached—and I sneak out unnoticed.

The stability of my relationship with Ayako has weakened recently because of (1) my inability to finance her trip home (I hadn't been frank about my situation, and she still thinks I can support her); and (2) her father's knowledge of our romantic connection. She asked me for ten thousand yen to return to Nagoya because her eighty-six-year-old paternal grandmother is in the hospital. She's too embarrassed to seek her family's assistance; they would be outraged to learn that she only has three thousand yen in her bank account.

She never addressed directly how a university student, with generations of dentists on both sides of the family, falls into such a predicament. I speculate that she's mismanaged this month's allowance from her parents on clothes and socializing. I certainly didn't get any of it. No wonder she's been tight about financial favors. Still, the announcement was overwhelming. It was like hearing that the local fire department had burnt down. I even wondered if she had used the story as a litmus test of my love. Upon learning that I'm also strapped for cash, she talked about going to the police for emergency money.

She'd ordinarily ask her father, but he has his own problems. In addition to his ill mother, he wants to divorce his wife over assets. He also threatened to place Ayako in a university closer to home, thanks to her involvement with a foreigner.

I wish I could have seen his face that afternoon when he rang her room and I answered the phone. Men aren't allowed in the small, all-women's housing complex in which Ayako lives. But the rule created the desire it intended to prohibit: many women invite their partners over in the late evening. I was still present at night to hear him browbeat his daughter by phone.

She has mastered the technique of crying without tears. Had she, weeks later, appealed to him for money to come home, he would have blamed me for her problems, and would have acted upon his threat to bring her home.

6

"Sex," said Shirley McClaine, "isn't really about sex, but is about something else." That something else in terms of my current relationships with women is power. Each thrust is a battle against doubt, fear, anxiety, and feelings of worthlessness.

Japanese women completely dominate my social life. I have hidden behind them to escape the harsh realities of the weak economy, and of an insular nation that looks down upon me with slanted, unsympathetic eyes. My instincts tell me to return to the States, head bowed, and *get a life,* as they say. But surrender won't go down well. My life here will improve—eventually.

I have insufficient funds to mix with employed men of my age and insufficient courage to deal with the truth. But today I surprise myself by accepting an invitation from a male acquaintance who rings me for lunch and conversation. Financially and emotionally isolated behind my four Japanese women, I want to talk to a man.

Jim told me to meet him at the American Culture Center's library. While I wait I see a Japanese man who interviewed me for a position I didn't get. I pretend not to see him, and am happy I wore a sports jacket and tie. Jim finds me, and we go to Mister Donuts. He shares with me his most valuable piece of information for the day: he's returning soon to the States, without his Japanese wife and five-year-old daughter. His trip is badly conceived. His plans are unclear. No jobs or interviews lined up. No responses from the law schools to which he's applied. No nest egg of money with which to return.

It gets better. While he is preparing to leave, his wife moves into a much larger apartment. I don't know what to say. All evidence suggests that they have parted ways. According to Jim, his family will follow in a few months' time. But I ask inwardly why would she invest more money—close to $2,000 a month—for a plush Tokyo apartment instead of saving for a move abroad? It seems that she's rewarding herself for the finality of their relationship.

I decide not to press the issue. It's none of my business. Jim, like me, has had some trouble landing a job. He only has sporadic, short-term assignments in the English-teaching business, which is a lot better than what I have. His wife's probably supported him through the rough periods. He hands me a bag of goodies that includes law school applications to Harvard and Columbia, a book titled *29 Reasons Not to Go to Law School*, and a manual on the LSAT, the standardized American examination for law school.

After our lunch, the sky is bright, the air is crisp, and the temperature is comfortable. In the Shibakoen district, I encounter a black male on the road leading to the main entrance of Tokyo Tower.

"I'm a talent," said the American, who has lived in Japan for ten years. That's typical Japanese English for television entertainer. But I read the remark as his euphemism for being in between jobs. Why else would he be walking the pavement, casually dressed and unshaven, in the afternoon of a workday? Japan is in a deep recession. Employment is hard to come by. In him, I hear myself. That's because I've been using similar lines for similar reasons: "I'm a copyeditor."

He approached me because he is so hungry for conversation in English, and during the first ten minutes, I can't squeeze in a word. He tells me how he created his duet. How he recorded a compact disc, which I can't buy in the stores. How he survived for nine straight months, without Tokyo work, by dating hostesses for their money and "using people."

I leave feeling like a therapist. He just wanted to psych himself up. I wonder whether his survival talk is prophetic. I don't think I can last beyond this month, let alone nine. "Dating hostesses," I repeat to myself.

# 7

The use of amphetamines is characterized by heavy breathing, dilated eyes, and profuse sweating. Waiting for an opportune moment to ask Kumiko for rent money duplicates those symptoms completely.

I delay telling her the butt-naked truth until after intercourse; that tranquilizing state of relaxation might help us both. Then, and only then, does it feel appropriate to share with her my troubles.

But the words fail to shape themselves in my mind. For a long time, I simply stare at the clock on the adjacent table, until I reach a point of mental suffocation. I clear my throat a few times. I move my tongue inside my dry mouth. I try to warm my cold hands. I inhale deeply.

Then, I slowly explain the whole situation to Kumiko's ear. I'm broke. Jobless. The tank is on empty. I need your help badly. If you love me as much as you claim you do, prove it through actions, not words.

She cries heavily, horizontally, in our hotel room. The force of her suffering moves me. One would have thought I had struck her with a belt. For the first few minutes of moans, I don't know whether her pain stems from a deep concern for my well being, or deep regret for having an affair with a poor man. But I do know one thing: if, for whatever reason, she declines to help me, I will demand and pawn the Rolex watch I bought for her thirtieth birthday, two years prior. That I have descended to such a level of hopelessness is extraordinary.

In the end, this isn't necessary. She promises to stand by me and fixes an immediate date to settle my short-term financial affairs.

The news removes the weight of uncertainty. And, as we lay lazily, entangled in each other, with her head resting in the space beneath my chin, and arms and body wrapped around mine like a cocoon, I use all my energy to keep my composure. Indeed, I am thankful for the room's darkness.

# CHAPTER FOUR

## Withdrawal

AT FIRST, I FELT ASHAMED and emasculated. But the missed-meal cramps relieved me of any contrition. I told myself how much those same women benefited from my kindness, years ago, and how much they genuinely wanted to help me. It no longer mattered much.

Collectively, their love refreshes me. For Western television programs, gossip, and Italian and meat dishes, I visit Nozomi—she's the host. For Asian food and culture, I visit Yoshie—she's the cook and the arbiter of local taste. For total relaxation, I visit Ayako—she's the therapist, who absorbs the kaleidoscope of my emotions, and allows me to use her nearby room for privacy. And for last-minute rescues from calamity, I pay a visit to Kumiko—she's the money.

With Kumiko's one-month backing, I enter the landlord's office and pay my rent on time and in cash; electronic transfers, checks, and money orders aren't options for guesthouse residents. The staff apologize for forgetting to tell me last month about a discounted rental fee, and they refund the balance of ten thousand yen.

Grin on my face, spring in my step, I go immediately to Kitazawa bookstore, in the Jimbocho section of Tokyo. There, I buy a biography on Alexander Crummell, the nineteenth-century Pan-Africanist, statesman, and missionary, who was also an intellectual and philosopher of language. I want to get one on W.E.B. Du Bois too, but decide to do so next time, when I can afford it. Besides, Crummell is the intellectual godfather of Du Bois.

I ring Keio University and learn about its intensive—and expensive—one-year Japanese-language program for six hundred and ten thousand yen, which is completely out of my range. I go to Barbington's tea shop at Isetan department store in Shinjuku for its lemon pie, but it's sold out. So I purchase some pound cake as a gift for Yoshie, who invited me over for dinner. She makes some surprisingly dry chicken, with broccoli and cauliflower tonight. But freeloaders can't be choosers.

## 2

Nozomi shows me the latest pictures of Michelangelo, her sister's cat. It had to be taken to the veterinarian to rid it of fleas, which its owner assumes came from a stray cat she allowed inside to keep it company. What strikes me is all the cat paraphernalia in the background of the photographs—stuffed kittens, feline posters, calendars. I wouldn't be surprised to learn that she has lingerie embroidered with cat faces.

I'm sitting in Nozomi's apartment, rewinding a videocassette of NBA basketball games that she's recorded for me. The whole space reflects her personality: the black leather sofa, dark gray cloth curtains, navy blue refrigerator, the large television, the framed poster of Robert Mapplethorpe's art, the gray concrete walls, the books of Andy Warhol, Fellini, and Italian cooking on the coffee table.

What's absent is even more significant. There are no flowers, no bright colors, no family portraits. It's what you might expect to see at a man's place. There's no emotional warmth here; it speaks of practicality.

She has always considered herself a step higher than other Japanese women her age. She visited museums while the other girls sang at karaoke boxes. She watched Hitchcock films while they watched goofy local comedies. She cooked fresh food while they ate precooked meals from convenience stores or fast-food restaurants. When she was twenty-two she dated a man twice her age, while other girls frolicked with boys who had yet to work full time for a year. Relinquishing her virginity was one of her priorities when she arrived in Tokyo from a rural town in Aomori, for her studies. Love wasn't necessary. She just wanted to get the thing over with.

According to Nozomi, Japanese business men of her generation pursue young—preferably between twenty-two and twenty-five—very slim, conservatively dressed women with shoulder-length hair and shy mannerisms. They prefer the mother figures and the infantile beauties. And she doesn't fit the type. They are threatened by her independence and commanding nature. They are bothered by her age—she's twenty-nine—not to mention her body. I think she's gorgeous. In the States, she'd need a bodyguard for her voluptuous figure. But, in Japan, her peers think she needs a personal trainer.

Society's idea of beauty has gotten to her. She's always talking about dieting. She wears a girdle, and buys special soap from China that's supposed to remove body fat. Behind her veneer of confidence exists a frightening sense of loneliness and a strong desire for a relationship. Before we met, she had spent most nights at home alone. There had been a couple of one-night stands, but she hasn't had a steady man in six years.

In her early twenties, she paid three thousand dollars to participate in a series of motivational seminars. The Japanese male speakers coaxed the mostly women members of their audience to dependence on these seminars, which they presented as a positive thinking program. The sessions were modeled on a pyramid structure, with each ascending level representing a new point of enlightenment. "Graduation" into a higher class required additional money, which she paid.

How stupid it all was. She could have saved a lot of money by investing in a few self-help books. But she seems to think that the meetings paid off. (Though, for a long time, her credit card company thought otherwise.) She's now earning more yen than a lot of Japanese male office workers by selling insurance. Without a doubt, her religion is capitalism.

Thinking about all of this, I failed to notice that the videotape has stopped. I press start, kick back, and watch the Kansas City Kings play the Detroit Pistons.

3

My American journalist friend Trevor decides to return to America after a five-year stint in Japan. I expect to hear that he had accepted a promotion, or a different position at a new company, or planned to enter some sort of professional school.

"I'm going kayaking," he sings above the chorus of Japanese voices at Maisen, the fried pork-cutlet restaurant, in Tokyo's Omotesando district.

Huh! I want to tell him that I'm busting my ass to find any

kind of job. I'm borrowing money from Peter to pay Paul, while you quit your high-paying one to go kayaking down the East Coast of the USA. Instead, I congratulate him for having the courage to chase his dreams. He even sees a book in the adventure. I feel the sting of envy.

He tells me about his list of giveaways. I pass on the worn sofa, the dated suit, the two-toned overcoat, the electric shaver, the portable radio, the bicycle, the dining table with two chairs (like I have the space for them), the rice cooker, and stop him at his four-year collection of *New Yorker* magazines. I'm so excited that no one else had claimed them; I pick up the two heavy boxes right after the meal and bring them home by taxi. Thank God we live near each other.

Besides my NBA games, I prefer to read. Watching television is no escape from attacks to my pride, manhood, or humanity. While scanning channels, I stop at a scene with a black male and a yellow woman. The guy says, in English, that he's so happy to meet her, it's his lucky day, and they should immediately go out for drinks. From a different room, a Japanese teacher and his five male students spy on the activity via a secret camera. I suddenly realize that this is Japan's idea of comedy.

After the black guy leaves to wash his hands, the woman asks for instructions by portable phone. The teacher urges her twice to invite him to a friend's house, but she rejects the advice. Then, suddenly, the man returns. His baseball cap is turned backwards. His high-top sneakers are thick and tightly laced. He wears a T-shirt with a tan vest and jeans. He has a goatee.

He escorts her by hand to a separate room. The act prompts the teacher to instruct his students to save her, and together they barge in the room. Each time the teacher tries to separate the couple, the black guy becomes more aggressive: he punches him twice, the impact of which is exaggerated by sound effects, and he puts his hand inside his vest once, giving the teacher a gangster gaze.

"She's my student," shouts the teacher, again attempting to rescue her. But the black guy is not going to allow anyone to come between him and a potential piece of pussy. He lifts a chair. And just before he could motion to strike, a program staff member, completely separate from the televised scene, enters the frame and tells him to stop. At that point, the black guy sheds his hostility. He grins for the first time. He apologizes, like a good boy, perhaps for bringing too much enthusiasm to the role for which he was paid. He leaves the set.

Some Japanese producers give money to black males to caricature themselves on domestic television. They attempt to reinforce the negative images linked to them, and to send fear into the hearts of local women, in particular. On another variety show, two comedians give a black male an "etiquette lesson" as he applies for a bride. They dress him in a handsome kimono for the occasion and then have him pose for the application's photograph. They tell him to squat and make a peace sign. Next, they place a gadget in his ear for directives and monitor his actions by video camera. He enters a traditional tatami-mat room, where an unaccompanied Japanese woman sits soundless as death itself, in elegant white garments, on the floor. He sits on the side of the table directly across from her. They make small talk and drink tea. Then, at the suggestion of the show's hosts, he does wild dances for her.

At the end of the skit, the comedians asked the live program's three women guests whether they could marry such a man. Two said that they could be his friend. The third receives thunderous applause from the studio audience after saying that she could never marry that kind of man.

I can't believe my eyes and ears. The unspoken issue, of course, relates more to race than manner. What sane person would say yes under similar circumstances? Blatant propaganda. Both "comedy" shows are tutorials in discrimination. Watching them gives me a headache. I look at my university degree, résumé, and published articles closely to remind myself that I am not what they wish to define me. I turn off the television, scribble in my journal, and go to sleep.

## 4

I withdraw further from contact with anyone—at least until I get very hungry. I prefer to lie on the futon, staring at the ceiling and listening to the noises around me and outside: someone singing karaoke, the opening and shutting of windows, the flushing of the toilet. I am consumed by desirelessness. I told Yoshie that I wasn't in the mood one evening and she asked me why I had come over to her apartment. I thought she was joking, but she forgot to smile.

The act of love requires effort. I have to think about the woman I saw on a crowded train the other day. The one who smiled at me. The one who wore a white blouse and thinly padded white bra, which revealed the brownish pink aureoles of her nipples. We didn't speak to each other. Only with such fantasies can I fulfill my role with the women in my life.

After we chewed and swallowed the evening's meal, and rinsed it down with red wine, she talked about two of her friends who date married men at their companies. One is twenty-eight, has a boyfriend in Okinawa, and is having an affair with a man with two kids. She doesn't expect him to leave his wife, according to Yoshie, she just wants to have fun. The other is thirty, and fell in love with a married man three years younger. She has a relationship with a man her age, too, and has been thinking about ending the affair.

Yoshie was introducing the subject of deception for the first time. Her sympathy for the women surprised me the most. I pressed her for her opinion.

"Sometimes, you can be in love with both," she said, parroting what she had presumably been told by her older girlfriends.

I misread her. I thought that she would have condemned unfaithfulness, without question. For that reason, I used to think that her sense of morality balanced me. But now I think differently. Her unexpected response, allied with my inner battles with poverty, added to my paranoia. How long will it take before she's influenced by her friends' behavior? She's been an active listener for so long. When will she yearn to become an active participant and find another man? A gift interrupts my thoughts. She gives me Kenzaburo Oe's *Silent Cry*. Then, she requests to see three of my articles. All of a sudden she's interested in what I have written. I don't ask why and she doesn't explain. Maybe she plans to submit them to an editor at the publishing company where she works, in an effort to help me find employment.

I know that I'm near the end of my sanity when I find humor in the comic book's sexist storyline. A group of high school boys try to rape a girl in a locker room. The principal enters, criticizes, and orders them to his office. He's now alone with the girl, and after looking deeply into her eyes, starts taking off his clothes. The girl stabs him in the stomach with a knife and flees.

I had become surly and rude with my girlfriends. A trip to

Barney's New York in Shinjuku for inexpensive scarves, and Mitsukoshi department store for chocolate, is to show my appreciation. Late White Day presents. I spend practically all my money, regarding the occasion as an investment. I have to spread out appointments over the course of a week.

I ring Kumiko and Yoshie for later dates. Next, I celebrate with Ayako whose room is the closest to mine. She wants me to take her to see a Japanese woman's piano trio at the Blue Note in Aoyama. But, then, realizing I can't afford it, she speaks of going with college friends on her student discount.

A little after midnight, I use Nozomi's spare key to let myself into her spare, cold apartment. We have been seeing each other three or four times a week for the past two months; she gave me the key for convenience and to persuade me to move in with her again. She returns home drunk at one a.m. Since I hadn't rung her the night before about today's plans, she went drinking with her colleagues. I meet her at the entrance as she removes her shoes unsteadily. Her clothes reek of tobacco. Her eyes are bloodshot, face pink. There's a tad bit of undigested food on her lapel.

"I got dressed up for you," she says, softly, in English, in the upper range of her alto, with extra stress on the last word. Her voice rises nearly an octave. The sentence smacks me in the face. My eyes flush. To save myself embarrassment, I tell her to make some tea.

I enter the bathroom and shut the door. Here, before the mirror, I feel a golf ball forming in my throat. The longer I look into the reflection's dark irises, the more I see my father. I'm becoming him, I thought. And, as I recall my mother's disappointment about my father's ways, in all of their strangeness and variety, tears slip down my face. Pain shoots through my chest.

"The tea's ready," says Nozomi, into the door, bringing me back from New York City. I turn on the faucet at full capacity. I clear my throat. I inhale deeply. Hold it. Then, I speak with as much chest resonance as possible.

"I'm gonna take a shower." I was aiming for a deep bass of a voice. But it sounded like I was taking a shit. Through bathing, I gain time to compose myself. I try to cleanse my mind of all those bad thoughts. A lengthy sleep follows tea and, the next day, a lengthy silence follows lunch and television watching. Then Nozomi speaks. "I have a girlfriend," she says, "whose friend works as a babysitter in New York City for a rich family. Based on her experiences, American men wish to marry quickly. But the friend is uncertain about the direction of her relationship. You know why? He doesn't have a good job, or any savings, and he's childish. No savings," Nozomi repeats, as if testing the pitch. "I never really thought about that," she adds.

From then on, throughout the months that followed, she would reveal her thoughts indirectly about marriage, and would become annoyed at counter suggestions. A scene from *Little Buddha*, which is the closest I've come to the study of Buddhism, made her defensive. In it, the narrator tells the protagonist that desire leads to suffering, and that he should avoid the diversions of women. At once, the warning reminded me of Circe's advice to Odysseus: Don't listen to the Sirens' voices unless he wanted to die.

Nozomi's immediate reaction to that scene's translation was to move some hair from the left cheek to the back of the ear: her sign of discomfort. Then, her eyebrows bunched into a slight frown. Afterward, she exhaled loudly and started mumbling to herself. She frowned for the duration of the film.

That's when I realized that her comments about a lack of savings and childishness were not addressed only to me. They were also part of a long internal argument with herself.

Although I regret how I've treated her, and I've apologized sincerely, she shouldn't worry about me popping the big question. Circe's warning is too much on my mind.

5

The simmering hostility of the times reaches a boiling point with a gas bomb on a Tokyo train. It kills six people and hospitalizes one thousand. Footage shows subway staff transporting pressed and crisp businessmen, in blue suits and starched white shirts, by stretchers. Other commuters, including a few women, sit on sidewalks in a state of shock, with handkerchiefs covering most of their faces. Some passengers have bloody noses.

Like the Kobe earthquake, the terrorist act distracts me from myself. It also highlights the nation's image of itself. A natural disaster is one thing. But a calculated attempt to kill innocent people in a "safe" country is quite another. Japan will have to come to grips with such violence among its own people—violence not at the hands of a "foreign presence," as they so often say—and the reasons behind it.

I start to think hypothetically. Were I employed; I might have been on the same train, at the same time, on my way to work. I feel, amid the totality of unemployment, a sense of relief about not having work. But I have to—repeat, *have to*—give someone here, one of my girlfriends, an emergency telephone number in case of a catastrophe. I *have to* get some life and health insurance.

CHAPTER FIVE

# The Maker of Illusions

IN 1921, T.S. ELIOT OBSERVED that "the chief danger about Paris is that it is such a strong stimulus, and like most stimulants incites to rushing about and produces a pleasant illusion of great mental activity rather than the solid results of hard work." I thought my time in Japan would lead to a trilogy: Asian experiences, observations, and interpretations. The goal, any goal, prolongs one's stay abroad. But years later no manuscript exists, not a draft, not even a paragraph. Each time friends hear about the proposed series of books on contemporary Japanese culture, surely they laugh among themselves later, after I am gone. Tokyo, strong stimulant that it is, made my self-gratification and rushing about seem worthwhile. Wasted kindness, wasted energy, wasted money.

In 1922, in her book *Etiquette*, philosopher Emily Post writes, "A gentleman does not, and a man who aspires to be one must not, ever borrow money from a woman, nor should he, except in unexpected circumstances, borrow money from a man." Shame on you, people would say. What kind of man are you, anyway, peddling sex for short-term loans of love, food, money? What kind of man are you, using that money to pick up different women, which leads to another cycle of poverty and begging. How low will you sink?

Your guess is as good as mine.

## 2

Kumiko wears a fresh bob-style haircut from a salon in the Aoyama section. We continue to do a lot of things together in my room, on Saturdays, the day her husband works late. Over dinner at Omotesando's El Torito, we talk about possible links between the religious group Aum Shinrikyo and the recent sarin subway gas attack. The news has become the most discussed domestic issue, and the TV is full of panel chats and programs. Kumiko's mother calls her every day after scanning the newspapers for additional information about the group and the incident. She recommends carrying around a wet towel, at all times, as a defense against another possible gas attack.

Restaurant staff dim the lights. A steady, machine-produced drumbeat fills the air. Light applause follows. Seven employees march to a nearby table holding a cake decorated with sparkling candles. Next, the voice of Stevie Wonder drowns out the chorus of Japanese conversations. The song was written to honor Martin Luther King, Jr. Most of the natives probably do not understand the lyrics, but they need only to recognize the song's refrain: "Happy Birthday to ya."

In the middle of the commotion, Kumiko hands me her wallet underneath the table to protect my manhood. I pay the bill, and, later, return her change on the elevator. During the walk to Meiji Jingumae subway station, she agrees to increase my debt to her until my first payday.

3

On a windy and bright Sunday afternoon, Nozomi mentions Yasukuni shrine in Kudanshita, where there is a pond of carp. We spend a lot of time indoors, she says. I attempt to romance her with a thirty-minute excursion in a rowboat, and to fulfill my own oarsman complex, but the experience proves humbling. It's hard to keep cool, when competing against a strong—no, a violent wind. Mother Nature succeeds in making me look weak. I ask Nozomi if we can go to the bookstore.

Natsume Soseki is regarded in Japan as the greatest novelist of the twentieth century. Yet before his fame he had suffered a nervous breakdown. He was studying in England, and eventually his poverty, isolation, and an identity crisis bred an acute sense of paranoia. About that time abroad, he later wrote that he can't think of a worse fate than being "followed through the world by farting detectives."

Enter the English-language book section of Sanseido in Jimbocho. Reading still attracts an unwanted audience. You peruse a favorite periodical. A stranger hovers nearby squinting his eyes toward the text, or bending his knees, head tilted, to see the book's cover. I normally react harshly when it happens. A Western man offers the day's advice: "If you have a self-conscious problem, keep it to yourself."

Nozomi prepares a Chinese dish for dinner. All except the sweet and sour chicken taste bland, but beggars don't complain. We rent Orson Welles' *Citizen Kane* and *The Name of the Rose*, adapted from Umberto Eco's novel. Yet, far more entertaining is the televised trial of John Wayne Bobbitt and his wife, Lorena, who gained her fifteen minutes of fame by severing his penis.

"He's so selfish," said Lorena. "He never waits for me to come."

## 4

Three morning knocks on my door from a representative of the guesthouse staff. He explains their plans to install a slam lock on the entrance door and delivers the new key. Finally, security. While exchanging keys, I tell him about the recent robbery attempt. The thief entered the house through the rarely locked front door, placed a call on the lobby's public phone, and then departed with my umbrella.

"He was Japanese?" the native worker asks. He raises his eyebrows in tandem with his intonation.

"Yes," I reply. "That man tried to steal my umbrella, but I caught him."

"You caught him?" He lifts his bony index finger toward my chest, awaiting confirmation. I nod. The worker looks away in silence, and fingers his moustache.

The Japanese tend to believe the propaganda about their country's safety, despite news reports to the contrary. Look under the tatami mat of Japanese society: AIDS, homelessness, malicious crime, drugs, teenage pregnancy, alcoholism, child abuse, bullying, poverty, under-education. Hardly a day passes without some egregious wrong appearing on the news. Here are a few.

Buddhist priest is arrested for raping more than 100 women.

A man shoots dead a doctor inside Tokyo's Shinagawa Station during the morning rush hour. The doctor operated on the man a year ago. The gunman attributed the killing to his operation: "He put something bad in me."

A fifty-four-year-old, unemployed man suspected of murdering five women tells investigators that he dismembered the bodies of three of the five at his home in Osaka.

A knife-wielding man in Nagoya is arrested on suspicion of stabbing to death a sixty-six-year-old man and his one-year-old grandson at a shrine in Toyota, Aichi Prefecture.

A twenty-nine-year-old doctor kills his wife and two children, after he incurs an enormous amount of debt.

A thirteen-year-old boy commits suicide, leaving a note that his decision is a result of persistent bullying by nine junior high school students.

These are not aberrations. They are reflections of the larger society. Ask any Japanese woman whether she would walk alone through any Tokyo park at midnight; and ask an American woman if she would walk alone through Manhattan's Central Park. They both will give you the same crisp no.

Let me not be misread. This is not about which country has a monopoly on crime. It's about deception. There is a Japan for the tourists and a Japan for the locals. If you don't speak, read, or understand Japanese, you will never know what's happening here. Instead, you will accept the image Japan presents of itself. Poor international news coverage preserves the illusion abroad that the Japanese can take safety for granted at home. Only when major catastrophes occur do we learn about and pay attention to the goings on in Far East Asia.

At the same time, Japan reinforces the crime-free image by convincing her citizens that outsiders are the enemy. Foreigners—not us—rob, cheat, kill, live in poverty, and spread diseases. Generations of Japanese residents go through life believing this story unquestioningly. It gives them a sense of superiority, and it explains their doubt and then horror when they realize that their negative image of foreigners is, just as often, an image of themselves.

## 5

Almost every day, an officer steps out of the police box on Omotesando Street and stares at me angrily as I pass. That's the Japanese equivalent of harassment. You'd think I had hit on his wife.

One day, as I am busy ignoring him, he steps into my path. We nearly collide; I have to dance sideways to avoid his shoulder. There is a vehicle parked on the street, and for some reason he has decided to go inspect it. He peeks into the window and returns. I am watching all this from a phone booth to confirm my theory: he just wanted an excuse to get in my way. As he returns to his police box, I step out and follow him. He is already chuckling at the other officer, but the officer sees me and his eyes widen. Five other officers dressed in blue uniforms draw closer.

In Japanese, I ask him soberly whether he has a problem. Is that how you normally respond to black men? Do you assume something strange? Another officer answers no. The intimidator remains silent with a blank expression. I go on my way.

## 6

I'm waiting for Kumiko between a small movie theater and Wave, the music store in the Roppongi section of Tokyo, where I first complimented her earrings. Her work prevents us from having lunch together. But in the narrow, concrete corridor that leads to the downstairs theater, she gives me an envelope of money, a tight embrace, and a kiss. Were it not for her kindness, I don't know how I would have survived the month. We walk together to Roppongi Station for the Hibiya line. I descend at Kasumigaseki, she proceeds to Hibiya.

From the envelope, I pay rent at the landlord's office, buy a steak and cheese sandwich at Subway, and visit Kinokuniya bookstore. While reading an article in *The Economist* about Louis Farrakhan's restaurant complex on the south side of Chicago, I spot a Japanese woman and black man beside the entertainment magazines. Leaning against the wall, they discuss in English an article in *Rolling Stone*. He's slim, dressed casually in cotton pants, wearing a baseball cap that gives him a hoodlum air. She's dressed in an aqua miniskirt suit: she has a wide jaw, shoulder-length hair, big breasts, muscular legs, and a bull's buttocks.

While the guy buries his head in an article, I make eye contact with the woman. Then, I pick up *BusinessWeek*. Overhear her ask his permission to look at magazines in a different area.

I admit, I have been bored. So I tear out the subscription card and write down my name and telephone number. I wait a few minutes before wandering over to the fashion section, where she stands reading *Vogue*, leaning against the edge of a cabinet of travel guides.

"Excuse me," I say. "You dropped this."

She examines the card with my telephone number and name in large black letters. She glances at her male friend several feet away. He is not paying any attention, and she exhales, "OK."

As I step away, she slips the card into her shoulder bag.

I would love to say that I approached her solely out of boredom and to validate or invalidate the conclusions I had reached about women. But I also wanted to test the limits. I really did not expect anything to happen, though. Never did learn her name until she called me.

Twenty-nine-year-old Yumi studied sociology in Virginia for three years. She now lives in Nagano, four hours from the capital, and works with her parents in their small inn. But she doesn't like it. She really wants independence like her younger sister, who works in Tokyo and lives alone in Saitama.

Three weeks later, we have dinner together in Ginza. She comes to town to watch her sister participate in a ballroom dancing contest at Tokyo Dome. Yumi does most of the talking: She's attending driving school, she may travel to the States to attend her graduation, she completed the course work in December, she craves company. It's been so long, she says, since I really talked with someone. Returning to rural Nagano after studying abroad was too big of an adjustment, and she is experiencing a reverse culture shock. She felt so free in the States. She enjoyed her anonymous lifestyle. She avoided other Japanese students. She wasn't bound by the rigid, unspoken, second-class laws of women in Japan. Nor did she feel totally bound by U.S. laws.

"I think for Japanese men it's much different," she says. "They can't wait to return to Japan. It's very comfortable for them here. They have status here. In America, they're just another minority. No special status or anything like Japan."

Hers is an excellent and remarkable kind of flirtation. We exchange some heavyweight romantic blows. She lets me seduce her with devastating speed. I spend almost all of my money the way I used to. I buy dinner and a hotel room with what should have been two weeks of groceries.

Damn! I need help fast. Is there a psychiatrist in the house?

Seconds before reaching orgasm, she screams, in English, "Oh my God." I almost pass out trying not to laugh. I assumed she'd say something in Japanese. I find myself wondering where she had learned that phrase and where she had learned to use it in an erotic context. Probably some video she watched with American friends at college. Maybe she thinks that's how all Western women respond; that's how you're supposed to do it.

In bed, she tells me that her boyfriend has other girlfriends, her mother is having an affair, her father has a drinking problem, and her family doesn't eat meat. They only eat leftover raw fish left by the customers. I believe that our time together is only beginning. But she enters and leaves my story like a thief. I can't call her because she lives with her conservative family. They will ruin her campaign to move to Tokyo if they learn about me.

I, on the other hand, share a phone at the guesthouse, where the residents aren't the most reliable message takers. And I'm hardly ever home. Yumi is able to reach me once. Yet, without explanation, we never see each other again.

## 7

Almost a year after my encounter with Yumi, I meet her boyfriend. On my way to an interview, in the Kudunshita district, I spot and acknowledge a fellow black male heading in the opposite direction. I always greet black strangers abroad, otherwise they think I am conceited or ashamed of my race. He wears a suit with a white button in the lapel that says "I Love Herbalife." Herbalife is a nutritional products company known for its pyramid sales scheme. He comes from Ghana.

After a few pleasantries, he tries out his sales pitch. "Do you take vitamins?"

"No."

"You know you really should take care of your health, especially in Japan. The food isn't that nutritious. Raw this, raw that."

"I'm thinking about buying them individually. You know, vitamin C, when I have a cold..."

"Why do that? Our tablets cover your whole body. They cover everything. You won't have to spend so much money on so many vitamins, when you can just buy one for all your needs." He continues with a lot of gestures, until I refuse to buy anything. At the sight of a well-proportioned Japanese woman, he changes the subject.

"You got to be careful with these women," he says. "They like messing around. They're really nice and sweet in the beginning, but they change. I'll never marry one. They change after marriage and children. They won't give you the sex, but they'll give it to the next man. They're so slick."

"I know what you mean," I said. "I saw this one girl at Kinokuniya bookstore who was with her boyfriend. And I gave her my name and number on a subscription card and she called me and we got together and everything."

"Really? I was with a girl in Kinokuniya once. The one in Shinjuku?"

"Yeah."

"My girl told me someone tried to pick her up with a number on a card, but that she threw it away."

We spend some time confirming her appearance and some biographical information, such as the Nagano Inn and the studies in Virginia. My heartbeat quickens. I remove my glasses with the weak excuse that something is in my eye. I expect his bruised ego will lead to a fight.

It doesn't. Though shaken, he comforts himself with an admission of having a harem of five other women.

8

Misery, as they say, loves company. How pleasing to read in the *Financial Times* a book review by Jackie Wullschlager of Joseph Frank's *Dostoevsky: The Miraculous Years*. In 1865 the Russian novelist, aged 44, "was a starving, broke widower, living in fear of the debtor's prison, denied any meals at his boarding house, and compulsively gambling on the roulette table the few modest loans with which his friends tried to help him."

In an act of desperation he signed a contract which, in addition to three thousand roubles, gave the publisher Stellovosky rights to all his works, published and unpublished, for the next nine years if he failed to deliver a novel a year. Dostoevsky had no other source of income.

A month before his deadline expired, in 1866, he hadn't written a word. He dictated *The Gambler* to a young female stenographer in three weeks, had the manuscript deposited at a lawyer's office, and beat the deadline by two hours. It was under that kind of extreme pressure that he produced, between 1865 and 1871, almost of all of his greatest work: *Crime and Punishment*, *The Idiot*, and *The Devils*.

Learning about the great writer's dire straits has a tranquilizing effect on me, similar to that of receiving a full-body oil massage. I am connected to an international fraternity of strugglers and survivors, people who, by inner energy alone, catapulted themselves to respectability. Viewed from that perspective, these hard times are a rite of passage, an examination in the eyes of those before me. If I hold on and stay strong, I will see the light at the end of the tunnel. If I surrender to the weight of unemployment, I will die.

9

I purchased the newspaper first thing in the morning for a list of Tokyo and Osaka job openings. The ritual has been an empty one for months, but I still respond to promising advertisements with a cover letter and a résumé. Sometimes I even send them by express mail or fax.

As I prepare one during lunch, the sounds of '70s soul music floats into my small room. Slow, heartbreaking tunes about love plunge me back to childhood: a world of churchgoers dressed in colorful oversized hats, ice cream trucks blasting their music box melodies, and happy kids playing endless games and causing endless mischief. I can still smell the aroma of greasy, crispy, golden brown, fried chicken flooding the house from the kitchen. I long for home and family, and the time when I was full of hope. During those days, we just assumed that the future would be brighter. And it usually was.

Most Japanese-owned radio stations play only trendy tunes, not the slow jams of my generation. I wonder whether the music comes from the room of another black person. I rush through the gates of the guesthouse, around a corner, and up the stairs to a used clothing store on the second floor of a small concrete building.

It's a cramped space, full of faded jeans and bright Hawaiian beach shirts. A young Japanese male in a Kangol hat stands alone behind the counter, next to an Aiwa stereo system. He saw a Tokyo concert of The Stylistics a few years ago, and started collecting their CDs.

I return home in the light drizzle.

CHAPTER SIX

## A Fifty-Two Week Low

JUST AS I THINK THAT LIFE can't get any worse than joblessness, in a country suffering its worst recession since the second
world war, I get arrested.

I drink one beer too many at a farewell party for my Ameri-
can friend, who's leaving his high-paying job for kayaking in the
States. I feel fake misrepresenting myself among the employed.
The back of my head still aches from sustaining a forced smile.
I'm not even a drinker. But everyone else is guzzling beer and I
don't want to appear odd.

Later, on my way home, I see a former colleague on a subway
platform.

His presence cracks the gates to a volcanic temper passed down
from my father. I walk over to him. He smiles and compliments
my haircut. I haven't had one in months. He examines me from
head to toe and smirks. I ask him whether he's been spreading
gossip about me.

"It isn't enough that I'm temporarily out of work in my chosen
profession. You seem to want me to leave the country."

He says something condescending and I don't like it. I don't like
this idea that he can mock me and then brush me off like a piece

of lint. I select a few words to let him know that rumors can lead to trouble. He puts down his bag. People around us are watching.

He steps forward, speaks louder and faster. Some saliva escapes from his mouth and clings to his lip. His rage and contempt infuriate me. I step forward, match his tone, and release pathetic comments.

Then, I notice that my right fist is returning in slow motion toward my body.

When I am myself again, the Japanese authorities are taking us by car to a police station, where I'm arrested for throwing two punches and put in a cell in the early morning hours.

I drew my expectations for prison from American movies and hearsay. I expect to be thrown in the slammer and sodomized. That's why, when the guard asks me if I want a shower, I pass. His laughter confirms my fears. The next day, I learn that inmates are only allowed a bath every five days.

My priorities reorganize themselves. I wish to walk through a park, inhale fresh air, and feel the sun's warm rays on my face. I will miss American pop and rock concerts at the Budokan in the Kudunshita area of Tokyo, as well as dates with friends. People will wonder where I am.

Were I employed, my second priority would be work. I would worry about lost money—not to mention, lost face—and how to present the situation to my company. I am lucky not to have that good fortune.

2

At 6:30 a.m., the start of the prison day, I meet my cellmates. They hardly resemble the bruised, battered, and scared men I expected. Nor do they have granite physiques.

The system names me Thirty-three. Number Thirty-one learned English while studying art in New York City at Parsons. He took a leave of absence from school to save money in Tokyo. He's tall, slim, with long arms, and has a full head of curly black hair, a light moustache, and a goatee on his square jaw. His tries to exercise a lot, though he should eat more, and he draws cartoon characters in his notebook to pass the time here.

"The first thing we do after getting up," he says, "is return the futon and blankets. When that's done, we vacuum the cell and clean the toilet." He folds a few tissues around his right hand, dabs them with water, and wipes down the toilet.

There's no way in hell I'm going to do that. Instead, I vacuum, the others sweep.

The guard brings an invalid's meal for breakfast: weak, hot miso soup, cool rice with pickles, and warm water in a plastic bowl to wash it all down. In between slurps, Thirty-one shares his story. A few months ago, he launched a miniature rocket from the crowded Shibuya district to protest the nation's financial greed and spiritual emptiness, which he believes has given religious cults an opportunity to become powerful, and also causes crime. On its return to earth, the rocket hit and injured people. He is in prison for a year and a half.

Then, there's number Fourteen: average height, stocky build, shaven head, and high cheekbones on a mostly expressionless round face. He spends a lot of his time looking through motorcycle magazines (he wants to buy a Harley Davidson), reading Japanese comics, which contain pictures of semi-nude models, and writing in a diary he keeps under his pillow. He doesn't speak English, but Thirty-one translates.

He's served six months of a three-year sentence for buying

amphetamines. He and two women drove to the drug spot for a purchase. On their way home, they saw the police siren and panicked. The police found Ecstasy on him and marijuana in the dashboard. The women, whose urine samples revealed traces of drugs, received six-month sentences for being first-time offenders.

I wouldn't be able to survive years in a cage. Yet these men live comfortably in a society completely different from any I've encountered. Not once do I hear them complain. Luckily, weaponless assault is low on the scale of crime severity. Both men remind me that mine is a minor infraction, and say I'll be out in less than ten days. "A few months ago, a Japanese guy was here for fighting," says Fourteen, "and he was released in six days." Even that seems like forever.

3

A duty officer from the U.S. consulate comes to make sure I'm being treated well. She explains some aspects of the Japanese criminal justice system. The idea of release on bail is almost unheard of for foreigners; police can hold suspects for up to twenty days while conducting an investigation and before an indictment, and lawyers aren't allowed to be present during a suspect's interrogation. "If you want us to notify anyone about your arrest," she says, "you must give us written permission to do so."

I decide against having my family contacted. I'm ashamed, and just want to serve my time and move on with my life. I also decide against having a lawyer before indictment because I can't afford one. Only after a formal charge can I receive a court-appointed one. Hopefully, my case won't go that far.

On the second day, I meet the public prosecutor who requests and receives from the judge a ten-day detention order to permit the police to continue their investigation. The most important issue for the Japanese police is whether I'm living illegally in To-kyo. Technically, I am; I don't have a sponsor. That ended once I lost my job. But all that matters to them is the expiration date on my visa.

They drive me to the guesthouse in handcuffs on day three for my passport. It's early afternoon. Residents must all be fast asleep, due to some late partying, and I am relieved not to see anyone. I rush in and out as quickly as possible, with a blue jacket covering my hands and one detective by my side, while the others wait out front.

They nod upon learning the visa expires in two years.

"Good job," says one cop, as we enter the car, "good job." Part of the compliment is for not giving them any trouble: they assumed I'd try to flee. He buys me a Fanta grape drink from a nearby vending machine. Now, he's inquiring about my free time activities.

I'm seated in the backseat, handcuffed, with an officer on each side of me, and two in the front, including the driver. It's hot. I haven't bathed in three days. Nevertheless, he asks about my taste in music as if we're co-workers. He actually expects me to relax and laugh. I feel so stupid for encouraging him with answers.

During a moment of silence, he asks the other detective in Japanese whether my room was clean.

"It was messy," his partner says.

4

Boredom takes on fuller meaning. The empty hours drive me close to madness, and I obsess over how I could have escaped capture. I really should have stayed home instead of attending that party.

Memory distracts me. I remember the years of having money in Tokyo, college in Paris, and even earlier times. Childhood and the taste of cotton candy.

During meals, prison guards watch me eat—staring, grinning. So much for privacy. So much for manners.

Later, after this chapter of my life ends, I will have deeper suspicions about how Japanese people regard black people. Kenzaburo Oe, the 1994 Nobel laureate, writes in his 1955 short story, *The Catch*, about a black pilot caught and imprisoned by some local Japanese villagers. They all look upon and treat him as an animal before eventually killing him. This is how the narrator describes the prisoner's first meal after capture.

> The Negro stretched out an unbelievably long arm. With thick dark fingers that sprouted bristles along the back, he took up the bottle and, drawing it to him smelled it. Then the bottle was tilted, the Negro's thick rubbery lips opened to expose great pearly teeth in two orderly rows like parts inside a machine, and I watched the milk being poured into the Negro's vast, pinkly gleaming mouth.

The narrator goes on to word his lips as "almost painfully swollen, like a ripe fruit bound round with a cord." His hair is "small, tight curls rising like sooty flames above ears pricked like a wolf's."

He has a "thick and greasy" neck, which "fascinated me each time it twisted to form tough folds in the skin." His body odor is "persistent and pervasive as nausea welling up in the throat, seeping like some corrosive poison into everything about it." The prisoner didn't just eat the meal. He "attacked" it. That's what they think of me. I'm their catch. That's why they spend so much time scrutinizing my eating habits. For them, those horrendous portrayals depict all black people.

For the past few months, I've been stripped of money, pride, human companionship, and now privacy. This point not only represents my fifty-two-week low in Japanese poverty, but the lowest low ever. The only things I'm left with are my imagination and fanaticism for survival. I regard detention as the ultimate phase in a long process of inner purification.

Women used to consume all of my time, just like with a lot of single, heterosexual men in their early to midtwenties. I had a critical zipper problem—low-minded inclinations, if you will. But here I don't think of them in the same way. They aren't as important as I thought.

Isn't it funny that no matter how bad life becomes we always try to find something good within it. We have native optimism. You can drop to the depths of hell, but still you'd attempt to look at the brighter side: well, at least, I'm alive. I imagine an ancient spirit guiding me through tests to make me understand life's worth. I can hear it telling me that surely there are more important things than hedonism.

I won't call any of my girlfriends for help. I suspect most would laugh at my calamity.

I find an article in an old Asian edition of *Newsweek* left by the duty officer of the U.S. consulate. The feature searches out the ingredients of genius by looking closely at human history's great minds. I'm drawn to a passage about the obsessive work habits of creative heavyweights in the arts and sciences. I, too, need to "meet inspiration halfway," I mumble to myself. Even when I'm tired and lethargic. I have to write these Tokyo adventures down. Maybe I can help someone avoid my mistakes.

5

The final issue of importance for the prosecutor is the amount of money I have stashed away at home. When I tell him none, he's not having it. He sets my fine at one hundred thousand yen, or about a thousand U.S. dollars, for throwing two punches. Kumiko comes to the rescue with money for the penalty.

My release will be tomorrow. The news lifts my spirits, and for the first time, I decide to join the other inmates during the exercise period. Considering the interminable sedentary time here, I really do need to work out.

I expect to enter a sweaty room with men lifting weights. But the only things they are lifting are cigarettes to their mouths and electric shavers to their faces. At the entrance, one of the guards holds a tableau etched with about thirty holes labeled with numbers. Two cigarettes for each detained smoker. I return to the cell, stretch, and read.

Once freed, the first place I visit is Aoyama Book Center in the Roppongi section to read the English-language magazines, and to feel connected again to the larger world. I walk there from near Kasumigaseki Station, on a bright sunny day, squinting at the strong light as if I were seeing the outdoors for the very first time.

Although I have only thirty-six yen in my pocket and a one-month old commuter's pass, I feel reborn. Too bad I don't look that way. Skin hangs off my cheekbones, thick curly beads of hair cover my face and neck, and my eyes are bloodshot. I've lost weight. But at least I have control over my life again. I thank Kumiko for her unswerving support by phone. I scrub my body into a bronze glow. I fall into a deep sleep.

CHAPTER SEVEN

## Reinvention

RALPH ELLISON ONCE WROTE that the most useful things in life don't always come from money, nor are they intentionally offered. True enough. If you had asked me whether I would have been able to survive an experience like detention in Japan following months of no money and no means to support myself, and not come out half crazy, I would have said no. I'm more resilient and tougher than I thought.

My first confidence boost came from Hawaiian-born sumo wrestler Akebono. His promotion to sumo's highest rank, yokozuna, made him the first foreign wrestler to reach that level in the sport's thousand-year existence. The entire nation considered such an accomplishment unthinkable a mere generation ago. His success within a frighteningly rigid Japanese structure, through wit, drive, and discipline, inspired me to forge ahead with my own endeavors. Each time he thrust an opponent out of the ring, and claimed yet another tournament win, pride and happiness energized me. He even claimed the crown over the crowd's favorite, a Japanese wrestler from blue-chip wrestling stock named Takanohana.

Another boost came from a technology advertisement in an

English-language telephone directory. I spotted it by chance. The caption of the small illustration stated that "you have to set yourself on fire" to thrive in any corporate environment. I married myself to that phrase. I believed those words had been written especially for me. I saw myself working at a smoking, cartoon-like pace, flames erupting, licking around me.

A few days behind bars was my most important motivator. It got me out of bed each morning and galvanized me into an exhaustive employment search, which resulted in a part-time teaching job at what I'll call the Language Academy, an institute specializing in foreign languages, supported by the Japanese Ministry of Education. The news of my acceptance was like champagne.

They offer me two separate jobs: one in the day, the other at night. I take both. The first is a three-month deal that requires me to teach four groups of university-aged students, twice a week, during the day, at the rate of six thousand, eight hundred yen an hour. The second is a six-month contract teaching business classes in the evening at a Japanese cosmetics company, four times a week, at the rate of nine thousand yen a lesson.

The day's exchange rate is eighty yen to the U.S. dollar. Do the math. That's enough to pay off my debts and prepare a move back to the States. Hopefully, my experience will lead to further opportunities, making my trip home all the better.

I was lucky. I just happened to call the school days before their advertisement was to appear in a local newspaper. I discovered their number in the telephone directory while calling scores of businesses for work. I owe my selection almost entirely to the academy's American dean, who swiftly arranged a meeting with the president, put in a good word, and informed me of the additional evening classes. Were Japanese staff empowered to make the decision, I would have gotten an interview and a swift rejection. They base their choices on a system devoid of substance.

The dean enjoys his work and the status it brings. He takes a long time telling me about his great-grandfather, who fled from Nazi Germany to Chicago before World War II. He is comfortable here, and Japan suits him—even though his brand new motorcycle was stolen a year ago from the complex he shares with his wife and children. After a long time, he gets around to the point. My job, he says, is the equivalent of four people's wrapped in one and the Japanese here don't like it.

While I'm signing contracts, a teacher with a British accent enters the office and shyly inquires about more work. The dean replies that if he pushes me in front of a train, there will be more available. The thought surely crossed the other teacher's mind: for earlier, when he saw me on the street, he ignored my greeting. Bet he doesn't feel so superior now.

Later on, when we're alone again, the dean moves forward in his chair, and leans in conspiratorially. "I'm not worried about what happens in the classroom," he says. "I'm sure you'll do fine. It's what happens outside of the classroom that worries me."

He doesn't elaborate; I don't ask for an explanation.

Outside of the classroom, I get a frosty reception from the full-time teachers. During unavoidable encounters, some snub, others scowl. They regard the school as their property and bitterly resent outsiders. They give themselves all kinds of airs. But once you strip away the superficial snobbery, you find them empty. Moreover, they know that newcomers from English-speaking countries will detect their pretensions fast.

2

Pre-lesson nervousness counters the post-hiring euphoria. The school doesn't have a training program for new staff. It assumes that everyone hired has experience. A Canadian man with two earrings in his left ear conducts the orientation, which consists of handing out roll books, texts, and briefly talking about term dates and potential student projects. He finishes with an invitation to contact him whenever we have questions.

I have a secret to confess: I've never taught. Never. My résumé shows a background in journalism, not education. I lied about my teaching experience during the interview. Decided that teaching nonnative English-speakers couldn't be that difficult. Now I have to reinvent myself into a teacher. I have to become one.

The evening develops into one of imperatives. Read Andrew Carnegie's *How to Win Friends and Influence People*. Remain in control. Understand thoroughly the teaching material. Work hard. Consider buying a ring to use as a wedding band: that way, the women students won't misread my intentions, and others will take me more seriously. Protect my personal life. Remember all things are connected. Don't cut off my moustache; I look too young without it.

Professionalism and friendliness will have to compensate for a lack of teaching skills in the beginning. That said, I'll prepare for the worst and hope for the best. But, first, I need a haircut.

While standing in central Tokyo before a rotating barber's pole with red, white, and blue lines, I feel fright sweep over me. A nearby mirror shows me that my hair has spread wildly down the back of my neck, and overall, the left side is longer than the rest. The more I stare at the reflection, the more my hair resembles the thick, long, bushy look of Michael Jackson at the peak of his career with the Jackson 5, in the mid-1970s. But mine shows neglect. My once-dependable ritual—shaping portions of it with my palms—cannot hide the hair's true state.

For several months, I have been convincing myself that I don't really need a haircut in Japan. What's at issue here is an encounter with a Japanese barber.

Meanwhile, I replaced my brush with my older brother's Afro comb—the one with the metal teeth and the handle like a closed fist. He predicted, with a wide grin at the airport, that I would need it.

You had to be well groomed in my neighborhood in Harlem. One's hairdo represented one's masculinity. The style, the barbers you went to, and cut itinerary unofficially determined your acceptance among your peers, or a willingness to be accepted. Old friends would wipe their eyes from laughter, if they could see my half-year's worth of outgrowth now. "My, my, *my*, " they would shout, with incremental modulations in tone, "that's a bird's nest, right there!"

New Japanese friends, however, compliment my coiffure. "You need lots of hair in winter to prevent sickness," one says. There's truth to that remark, but I know better.

Other men from English-speaking countries say that, amid all kinds of foreignness here, their hair connects them to the locals. Getting a haircut makes them feel at ease under a foreign barber's hands. But I don't have that luxury. From the moment I stepped onto the ground of Japan's Narita Airport, I was a long way from any barber who knew how to cut my texture of hair. The few black people I know in Tokyo adjust by having dreadlocks or Afros or perms or braids or bald heads.

I have always frequented only black barbers—even during college in Paris.

Japanese scientists can invent gadgets that are far ahead of their Western equivalents. Crime is lower here than in other industrial nations. Japan has many virtues, but I doubt whether a Japanese barber can cut my hair as I like: no line in the front, a square back, a little off the sides, and none off the center because it's thinning there.

Based on the wide-eyed, stone-faced look of the Japanese barber staring at me through the window, I think he feels as uncomfortable as I do.


3


Inside, three barbers are talking about a Sumo wrestling match the day before. They are dressed in white tops and black pants, and when the door closes behind me, they rush to a corner of the room, where they decide who shall approach the task. In the interim, I am politely offered a seat.

Five TVs entertain customers with an American science fiction film, while a high-tech stereo system lightly plays a recording of an American pop melody. Tonics, aftershaves, powders, razors, and various clippers are lined up on the shelf beneath the mirror. A wooden stand filled with Japanese comic books and magazines sits near the entrance. One man keeps his eyes closed while lotion is applied to his face. A woman barber massages oil into another man's scalp.

As I wait my turn, I remain divided over whether I should cut my own hair; doing so would make me self-sufficient. But the last time I tried, I had to shave my head clean to hide the bald spots.

"Customer," says a barber in Japanese. I look up to see a slim man with short, gelled hair waving me over. English-to-Japanese dictionary in hand, I explain in detail the kind of cut I want. The barber wraps me in white cloths like a dead Samurai. He then proceeds to style my hair, timidly. The slow combing exaggerates the hair's thickness.

I feel sorry for him. His hand is shaking. When he gestures to his fellow barber for further instructions, I realize that I'm in trouble. He is a trainee, and he swaps customers with his mentor, who tells me that he has a black client who comes to the shop regularly. The barber then assumes that I too want my hair closely cropped.

I knew I should have cut my own hair, but how could I blame him. American films and music videos and U.S. military recruits based in Japan have made the style popular.

He's holding a razor blade in his right hand. I never did figure out the Japanese word for ingrown hairs: that bumpy post-shave state experienced by many men with woolly locks. Next, he grabs a pair of shiny scissors. I suggest clippers. Throughout this ordeal, an additional three barbers watch closely and carefully, making me feel like a guinea pig.

In the U.S., the function of a barber shop has never been solely to cut and style hair. In the best sense, it serves as a center of news, bets, entertainment, scandal, gossip, and diversions. But I don't intend to interrupt Sato-san's intensity, which is understandable, since I have enough hair for three separate cuts. Indeed, the task would be a challenge for a gifted Harlem barber. So, we approached the job together: step by step, inch by inch, snip by snip.

I retrieve my eyeglasses to find that the result, though only fair compared with one at home, looks much better than my previous attempts. I'm not used to the head massage afterwards, but it is nice; I was tense. I take a last peek in the mirror, and the longer I study the hairdo and the new contours of my head, the more pleased—and relieved—I become. The barber is smiling with his mouth closed and nodding in approval.

It is at this point I realize that being here is about more than just getting a haircut. It's about taking the fear out of exploring new cultures, and finding ways to break down the distorted images of each other that stand between us like walls. The process removes you from that comfort zone, but you return to an improved place, happier than you were before.

I give Sato-san the comb with the metal teeth and the closed fist as a souvenir. He gives me a discount, and urges me to return. I pay the bill, make a future appointment, and shake his hand. At the door, the staff thank me in Japanese and bow in unison.

4

I model my classroom style on Sidney Poitier in *To Sir, with Love*. His character, Mark Thackery, is an engineer who is teaching because he can't find a job in his main field. So, he works as a teacher of challenging, working-class students. He lacks teaching experience, but accepts his posts to make ends meet. He looks constantly for jobs in his field, and lives far from his hometown, in an environment foreign and hostile to minorities.

We both are outsiders, as Mary M. Dalton puts it in her book, *Hollywood Curriculum: Teachers in the Movies*.

I eye Poitier's wardrobe—dark suits and matching ties against white shirts. Timeless. I don't have many suits, but will wear solid-colored blazers with dress slacks. I bought the jackets at secondhand shops in Greenwich Village, a while back, but they look presentable and wear well. That style will certainly contrast with the other more casually dressed teachers. I adopt it for no other reason than to draw attention away from my weaknesses in the classroom.

For demeanor and ways of managing a disruptive class, I take notes on how Poitier's character almost always remains calm and collected during the lessons. He's in control of his emotions, a trait I will have to perfect. He treats his students with respect— even though their behavior usually warrants a more aggressive approach. He comes off as soft, but he eventually wins his students' respect and cooperation.

In the real world, I don't have any naïve, Hollywood-ending wishes for my job. I just want to do it well, create a good impression, and, most of all, save enough money for the next chapter of my life.

5

The textbook is composed of units on light conversational topics, such as music, movies, and sports. All units have the same structure, with the aim of developing students' grammar, followed by pronunciation, listening, and fluency skills. It doesn't come with a teacher's edition, which would have recommended how to present the material. So I do each exercise as it appears in the book, without deviation. No games. No props. No chances to allow the students to generate their own questions. Limited role plays and pair work.

It's dreadful. My class is as boring as watching paint dry. But I get no complaints from management, and no one observes my classes after the first day, an easy lesson on introductions. Students spend most of the time asking me the kind of questions one might expect in Japan on the first meeting: What's your blood type? Do you like sushi? Do you like natto? Are you married? How old are you? Can you speak Japanese? Where are you from? Does everyone have gun in America? (They tend to drop indefinite articles.)

A few class clowns break the monotony with unexpected questions like "What kind of girls do you like?" and "Are you big?" I think the latter one means muscular, but then he points to my crotch. I ignore him and the laughter.

I discover that my students' age and occupation determine their expectations of me. Full-time academy students want their teacher to be an entertainer, counselor, and occasional friend. The business students, however, have specific goals that they want to achieve in English in a limited period of time, like speaking on the phones, negotiating, writing business correspondence, making small talk during a business lunch, and making reservations.

At night, on our way to the train station, the person responsible for selling courses to the cosmetics company speaks honestly about my first class, which he observed, and the students. "You'd make more money and would be a better teacher," he says, "if you spoke Japanese." Tell me about it. "You may not want to push the students so hard, either. Remember that they are the customer. It's OK with the daytime students, but the business students are the customer, so you don't want to push them too hard."

He describes them as stupid, and the English-conversation business as a racket, after his third gulp of Kirin. "You know what? The best Japanese students work at banks and trading companies."

And who is he, who is giving me advice? A former salesman for a skin care business who used to live in Los Angeles as a university student.

According to Mr. Kodera, most students' spoken language skills don't improve significantly because the class size is too large and many are lazy. Those who become fluent find that they can't automatically land a job at a foreign company as they had thought. Many can't find a job that allows them to speak English. A few can't find work at all. So, in the end, their parents have spent an enormous amount of money—indeed, they could have sent their kids abroad for less—and the students accept jobs outside their chosen fields, in companies where they speak only Japanese. Whatever. As long as my salary enters my account on time, the school can hustle potential customers however they want. I'm not here to develop great Japanese orators of the English language; I'm here to help them achieve some modest aims and pay off my debts in the process.

# CHAPTER EIGHT

## Transition

AFTER A HARD DAY'S WORK, my evening students can be vicious. A few of them keep up a running commentary on me, in their own language, as I write on the board. Blackness is my secret weapon: no one thinks that I can understand Japanese, so they speak freely. I pretend that I'm monolingual to eavesdrop. Two women speak about my need for a toupee (so what I'm balding), tie clip (I'm working on it), cuff links (I can't afford them), a nose-hair remover (I'll take care of that after class), and cologne (I do wear fragrances, lightly).

One of the older students joins them in the fun. He says that I only have blue suits. Thanks for noticing. When it comes time for those comedians to speak, in English, I ask them the hardest questions, correct them the most ferociously, and assign them the most demanding segments of the group's homework. I take pleasure in watching them sweat.

Overall, as a foreign teacher, I receive my students' obsessive attention—on everything but my lessons. If I drink a Coke, they want to know whether it's more popular than Pepsi in the U.S. If I open and read a letter, they want to know whether I live near their office. If I wipe my brow, they ask me whether I'm hot. If

I rub my eyes too much, and they become red, they think I've been drinking. If I go to the bathroom, some male students will enter as I unzip. They want a bonus lesson. They want to see for themselves. Is it true? I move away from the urinal to the toilet and close the door behind me for privacy. When I reenter class, several people lower their eyes toward my crotch for stains. This bunch is something else.

## 2

The day's lesson centers on using simple past tense structures to talk about last weekend. One woman explains that on Saturday someone stole her wallet from her bag while she played an arcade game. She lost 5000 yen, credit cards, everything. So much for the myth of Japanese safety.

Another student says that work was slow at his part-time job at Mister Donuts, thanks to the heavy Sunday rain, which gave them time to play some kind of quiz game. The loser had to eat a donut for each error. He ate sixteen donuts. So much for company loyalty and the protection of profit.

When a third one says she went to Yokosuka, a U.S. military base, to visit her boyfriend over the weekend, her classmates smile. They can imagine the particulars. She says she enjoyed herself.

An outspoken student says she had a disastrous job interview. Male staff commented openly about her leg size during the meeting. They asked her to stand up, remove her suit jacket, and turn around to check out her figure. Was it for a modeling job? No. It was for a secretarial position. She refused with silence and stillness; the staff showed her to the door. Such kind of sexual harassment, she says, makes her hate looking for work. Some of her women peers nod their heads in agreement. Her male classmates avoid eye contact.

In the evening, I deal with some pettiness at the cosmetics company's classes. "You speak English nicely for an American," says one of the upper-level students. Ouch!

3

My schedule doesn't encourage camaraderie among teachers and students. There are no parties, trips, or discussions in a common area. There is only enough time to work and leave. Adjacent-room teachers, though, sometimes chat in between or before lessons.

A daytime student approaches me after class. She invades my private space—arm's length, or a little closer—to tell me about a Bon Jovi concert over the weekend. I don't know what to say. I'm surprised by her closeness and the absence of others. I don't want her to catch me stealing a glimpse of the deep cleavage that her low-cut dress exposes. So I force a few comments and quickly turn to my briefcase and papers. She stares at me, perhaps senses my uneasiness, and without another word, departs.

I share what happened with Todd, the part-timer in the next classroom. He says it takes place all the time. "They wait until graduation to go after teachers." Our favorite subject, though, is discrimination.

He tells me about a Japanese staff member in the recording room who gave him a hard time about allowing him to borrow a cassette. He thinks that we probably wouldn't have been hired were they making the decisions. Todd was turned down twice for a position at this school.

"They even turned down a brother with a degree from Harvard," he says. "I lived in Japan for eleven years and for seven, it was hard finding a job. I mean, I used to live in a room, and it got so bad where after interviews, I'd ask Japanese employers directly: 'Do you have a policy against hiring African-Americans?' And this one cat said, 'Yes.' I was like *damn.* "

On that note, he jumps up dramatically, rushes to the wall, and mimes doing pushups.

He's wearing a tight brown suit with suede, mustard colored shoes he bought on the cheap. They resemble pimp shoes. He's tall and clean-shaven. He has medium-length curly black hair, a small button nose, and a friendly smile. His business card says "music producer" under his name. I learn nothing in detail about his background, but I hope I will learn more soon, as his friend.

## 4

I usually hear writing ideas when I'm least able to remember them, in dreams. I'm alert enough to know that my room's cold, but too exhausted to do anything except sleep. I almost always forget those dreams, but this morning was different. I repeated the recollection over and over again, and woke thinking about Henry James's short story, *The Madonna of the Future.*

The story is narrated by an old man who tells a tale set in his youth at a dinner party. There, he met a young American painter who associated the highest achievement an artist can make with the illustration of perfect womanhood embodied in the Madonna and child. The painter is the object of ridicule for having been at work on his masterpiece for twenty years, though no one has seen it. When the narrator finally sees the painting, after the painter's death, it is totally blank. In the end, the American dies, having wasted his life preparing himself to create great art.

I drifted for the rest of the day in a deep depression. I saw myself in the story, and feared that I would end up as a man who spoke of his plans, but never acted upon them.

5

Kumiko has just returned from a business trip to Seoul. Her trip coincided with the 50th anniversary of the end of WWII. Here, former foreign minister Michio Watanabe tells a party gathering that Tokyo took the Korean peninsula without a struggle. He's quoted in the local press as saying that "it was a treaty formed peacefully, in which no words about colonial rule were written." In response to those comments, South Korean protesters set aflame an effigy of Watanabe before the Japanese embassy in Seoul. After the local police put out the flames with a fire extinguisher, the protesters kicked and poked it for good measure. Kumiko says police were everywhere and that restrictions prevented her from even taking pictures of young women. (I wish similar restrictions existed in Tokyo: three different people took my photograph last week.) Men from her company all received calls from Korean prostitutes. "They seem to like that," she says.

Her next foreign business trip is to the U.S. At dinner, she pulls out a travel guide and turns to a detailed map of Manhattan. "Where do you live?"

Blood rushes to my head. My heartbeat races. I release nervous laughter. I point to the upper west side of Central Park. My fingernail indents 89th Street and West End Avenue.

"No, I'm joking. My family live there, actually," I say, and redirect her eyes to the area north of the park, Harlem.

"Oh... It's a nice area, near the trees," she says.

I can't wait to return home. I'm so ashamed for feeling embarrassed about my humble origins. I have to rid myself of this notion that there is something wrong with my working class background. At the same time, I'm hurt for misrepresenting myself. I think of George S. Patton's axiom: "I don't measure a man's success by how high he climbs but how high he bounces when he hits the bottom." Yet I know that Kumiko will investigate the neighborhood. She'll realize that I'm not the man she thought I was. *I see why he has remained in Tokyo for so long,* she'll say to herself. *Who'd want to return to a place like this?*

The difference between the Tokyo employed and the unemployed is narrow, regarding their lifestyle. Everyone has a small home—even homeowners. If you are poor, you simply spend as little money as possible. You choose convenience store food or homemade meals. You rent a video instead of going to the movies. You open the window in the summer instead of using an air conditioner. You go to a public gym for exercise, rather than join a sports club. You stay home during national holidays, and don't take a trip.

Thus, domestic joblessness and underemployment don't come at the same social cost as in Manhattan. If you aren't gainfully employed in New York City, you don't fit into its culture of consumption. You'll feel inferior for your inability to keep up with what everyone else has and does.

6

The more I work, the more thrifty I become with my free time. I prefer to lay alone on the futon. I read. I reflect. I write. The path toward economic independence makes me less willing to put up with unhappy and unhealthy romantic ties. I no longer feel com-pelled to continue relationships with the women in my life, at least not in the same way.

An article on Eazy-E, the American rapper who died of AIDS, stresses the urgency of making some radical changes in how guys like me live and define manhood. The old conventional wisdom suggested that gays and drug users were among the highest at risk for the world's most dreaded disease. But the HIV virus can be contracted by anyone—straight, gay, suburban-ite, rich, poor—and if you stop and think about it, it hits you like a bombshell. You used to think that rappers exaggerated the frequency and variety of their after-hours adventures. Now you know better and listen differently to their lyrics. You think about the risk-reducing benefits of marriage. You think about celibacy. You think about spirituality.

Nozomi says a lot of Japanese people think that they are ge-netically different from other human beings on the planet, and, as long as they date and marry their own kind, they could never catch the disease. As for spirituality, what's that? She's an atheist. It's what people do that's more important than any intangible thing. Yes, what people do.

Sex—the kind that's unemotional and stripped of intimacy—ru-ins everything. I've grown indifferent to the act, and compare it to exercise rather than anything positive. The moment I reach sexual satisfaction, I want her to leave or to turn into a pepperoni pizza. I can trace almost every catastrophe in my life to the distractions of lust. Now that I'm employed again I want to redefine those relationships. I can be a better friend than partner, I think. I feel so guilty for having nurtured unfaithfulness as a way of survival. Deep inside, I hope that they leave me of their own accord. If they find someone else willing to spend for their love, I won't mind in the least.

On second thought, it would probably hurt me if any of them did. Sexual and emotional addictions are difficult to break. Maturity can be a rough and painful path, but I commit to beginning a more productive relationship with myself. I will stop glutting myself on passion, and develop the mind.

7

I learn to appreciate new things—art, dance, and cooking—to become a better friend with the women in my life. I make an effort to expand our number of small-talk subjects, and to contribute more to conversations about their most enthusiastic fascinations. I want to possess and build on the kind of intimacy that people often have *before sex*. This way I can shift our time together away from the bedroom to a flirtation of the mind. It was from that perspective I joined Nozomi to see William Forsythe's dance ensemble at the Bunkamura Theater, in the Shibuya section of Tokyo—a performance that would have otherwise bored me.

It takes three consecutive paydays to settle the bulk of my debts and to bring stability within reach. My girlfriends gave freely and thoughtfully, and rallied me with kindness, love, and affection; and now they say payback is totally unnecessary. They made me feel special and unique. They convinced me that I was worth their love. I really can't price what they did. So, after I insist that they accept the cash, I take each woman out for a special dinner. I present them with a different gift from Tiffany's to show my appreciation.

A series of arguments with Nozomi, however, makes our incompatibility clear. Her love seeks to seal out the forces that keep me going, including the ones that are only just awakening in my mind and spirit. I tell her I need a life and friends away from her, for my intellectual growth. What I don't tell her, in so many words: Her love produces inaction, passiveness, late nights, late mornings, last-minute work preparation, a total affliction of mental numbness. We watch television, videos, talk about nothing special, and fuck every chance we get. Excuse my English. Multiple that lifestyle by ten, twenty, thirty years. The result is death. Slow death. Someone sitting on your shoulders at every turn, getting heavier. Someone whom you can't even trust. She may leave you for another man with more status and wealth.

Many men search for possessive, lonely women. They make you feel important and needed; their attention fills some sort of infantile void. But I want to learn how to manage adult responsibilities, by myself, before I can think seriously about cohabitation. Only then can I hope to get over my fear of commitment.

But Nozomi wants even more than that.

"Could you marry me in the next two or six months? You will leave Japan soon and then I will not have a chance." Her tone is an argumentative, hair-splitting soprano.

When we lived together, a while ago, she once looked at all of my belongings, piece by piece, for any hidden (her word) information, after I departed for a job interview. Unluckily for me, she learned when my working visa expires. Then, she laughed about my situation with her closest friends.

I explain that I can't marry her now, especially under pressure. Who does she think she is, anyway, trying to push me around?

She says, "I'm old and I don't have much time." From the way she describes her age, you'd think she was getting hot flashes and going gray. She's thirty. Age, not love, is her primary motivation.

"What's love got to do with it?" she demands. She believes that the reason you marry is less important than what you do after marrying. She threatens to have an arranged one, if I don't commit. Yet, I don't budge one millimeter. It's true that in the past I even considered marrying her, but she cured me of that.

When these tactics fail, she spreads a layer of romance-novel fantasy on the argument: "I wanna have your baby. I wanna have your baby now."

I worry that the neighbors may hear her screaming.

She has tried to entangle me in a premature marriage already. She often told me that I didn't need to use condoms with her. And she'd become angry afterwards when I insisted on using them.

On my way out, she tells me never to call her again and slams the door. I become physically ill following our break up. But my desire for independence overwhelms my desire for more time with her. As for the other women, I see them less thanks to busier workdays. The lack of time, combined with the recession, eats away at those relationships. Ayako returns to her distant hometown after losing her job. Yoshie is set on becoming an adult, her word for becoming a wife and a mother, but her hopes for me are tinged with disappointment. She starts a relationship with a married man. Kumiko says of her husband, "His condition is getting worse and I want to help him as a friend." She divorces him and moves into a new apartment with her mother.

CHAPTER NINE

## Stability

A STUDENT SPEAKS WITH ME about his failing grade. He thinks that his class participation should boost it to a D. It doesn't matter to him that he failed all the tests, including the final; that he didn't participate; that he often did homework the day of class, in class; that his overall attitude is undermining his request. But no, he "want D." He loses any sympathy I might have had for him by brushing his pencil against my shirt, leaving a faint mark. He didn't even apologize. I explain for the last time that I will not change his grade and walk away.

Now that the course is done, I choose job security over uncertainty and accept a full-time position with a school I'll call English International. The school provides Japanese immigration with the appropriate paperwork to get me another working visa. The Language Academy, on the other hand, only gives short-term work without sponsorship. I need a sponsor to be legal—without one, you can't rent an apartment, join a sports club, get a phone, or open a bank account. A few aliens solve the sponsorship problem by marrying into the culture. Others overstay their visas and live here illegally. Many just go home.

The rest of my part-time contract finishes in four month's time, after which my plans had been uncertain. I had thought about leaving Japan for a few days, so that I could return with a 90-day tourist visa, and save a couple of thousand U.S. dollars by completing the contract. Then, I would have returned to the States.

But one week before my visa expires, the full-time job offer comes. I feel like I am on history's agenda. If I continue to make sacrifices, I think, and realign myself with the universe, good things will happen.

2

I begin training for my new job. We learn to explain all the grammar covered in the books we will use in our classes. We learn the difference between first, second, and third conditionals; and we have to regurgitate the information at the drop of a dime, lest we embarrass ourselves before customers and, in turn, tarnish the reputation of the school. And we can't do that.

A big-boned, red-haired Australian woman with silver-framed glasses invites the five of us into a classroom with comfortable sofas. We sit in a semi-circle around her—the result of passing two written examinations, two interviews, and a model lesson before staff. She explains the first day's agenda in broad strokes. We fill out administrative forms. Before getting into the nitty-gritty, she wants to conduct a simple grammatical test, she says, and pulls out a sheet of white, A4-sized paper from her briefcase. She points to one person and asks for an example sentence of *can*, as possibility, not as ability. Each subsequent person gets a different request. As she makes several rounds, as each potential teacher stumbles, stutters, or stares at the ceiling, hoping for an easy one. You feel the temperature rising. You can't laugh at the person who erred on explaining the difference between "for" and "since" because you can't explain it intelligibly yourself. But you know it, though. You really do. Just can't explain it. Her aim, she says, isn't to put us on the spot, but to draw attention to the importance of class preparation. She wants to give us an idea of what's to come, the kind of lessons we'll teach.

And that was just day one. Will they demoralize us to the point of quitting tomorrow?

The amount of information was a lot to cram into five days. Hardly had time to assimilate any of it before they scheduled me for a class full of smiling students. But that kind of intensive grounding in their approach to English teaching was valuable. The sessions taught us a great deal about ourselves, too. Time, diligence, and practice made us all more adroit teachers, differentiating function and form, meaning and usage, simple past and present perfect.

3

At my new school, the native-English-speaking teachers as well as the Japanese staff are all friendly toward me. They invite me out for drinks; they share their personal information; they ask for my opinion on certain lessons. I detect after a few weeks that I am happy—an emotion for which I was totally unprepared. I actually look forward to coming to the office.

Meet American Greg. As senior teacher, he manages the educational aspects of the school in Tokyo's Shibuya district. He serves as a liaison between sales staff and teachers under him. He is also a broadcast system for the head office, and briefs us at our daily meetings. He talks to me about the NBA. I offer to bring in a videotape of one of the NBA championship games. (Ass kissing never hurt anybody.) He says that he had lent a tape of the All-Star game to a friend, who moved away without returning it.

"But I trust you," he says. "I don't expect you to move from your place," but "I might get thrown out."

He's dressed in a cheap white shirt printed with flowers, and wears no undershirt. Chest hair escapes from the top button. He hails from Nebraska, where he played linebacker on the state college's football team. He's about six-foot and stocky, and has freckles, a square jaw, and a cleft chin. He's down-to-earth and likes to joke and gossip.

Head teacher Jennifer calls to share the amended results of my final schedule. She also asks whether I could work on Friday, normally my day off. Although I have absolutely no time to prepare lessons, I accept without a fuss.

At the school's evening meeting, Greg tells me to be careful in dealing with Jennifer. You give her an inch, she takes a mile. You may have Saturday off and she will call you to work. If you work on that day, she may ask you next about working on your scheduled days off a couple of times a month.

What Greg doesn't realize, and what I never admit, is that I don't have the luxury to refuse work. I will accept every offer, every extra chance to earn more money, unless I am sick, or have another job scheduled on the same day.


4


Fridays after work are synonymous with drinking until your liver pleads for mercy. I'm sitting in a Japanese-style bar with three Americans, an Australian, a Canadian, and a Scotsman. The usual locker room banter dominates the conversation: sports and cock tales, complaints and gossip.

When I worked on a much higher rung of the occupational ladder, I held unfavorable opinions about English teachers. I had adopted the popular misconception that any person from an English-speaking country with a pulse could land a job teaching their native tongue in Japan. How wrong I was—at least about the more reputable, more competitive schools. Sitting around this table are some teachers with backgrounds I never associated with the English conversation business. Indeed, many of these guys could earn a lot more money elsewhere.

American Roy worked for Goldman Sachs Japan prior to joining EI. Why would he leave? He says he got feed up with the long hours and feeling underappreciated. "My boss used to leave the office at about 5:30 p.m. every day. And he'd always leave a big pile of work on my desk to be done by the next day." Additionally, he says that his colleagues left him off the invitation list for all social events. Headquarters asked him to stay another year before returning to the U.S., but he couldn't take the stress, the long hours, and the isolation anymore, so he quit. He's using this job to sort out his future. He plans to get an MBA in two year's time.

Scottish Ian followed religion at the University of London's School of Oriental and African Studies. He's here to take a break from the grind of a regular job, and is collecting data for a book he's writing on some stained glass windows at churches in Kyoto.

American Alfred was a young lawyer in Washington, DC prior to coming to Japan to study Aikido full time. Why would a graduate of Duke University School of Law give it all up for the classroom? This is how he puts it: "I got tired of having to pull the rabbit out of the hat everyday."

"It's nice if you like getting dressed up," he says, "eating out at fancy restaurants all the time, and feeling important. But I always wanted to study Aikido in Japan. I always wanted to develop my spiritual side. I thought I might as well do it while I'm still young and single." He's thirty-two. He goes to the dojo three to four times a week. His goal is to enter and complete an intensive, one-year training course for the riot police. After that, maybe he'll teach Aikido in the States.

Australian Neil, the computer whiz, has different reasons for being here. "You guys are too serious. It's the pussy, man. The pussy and the money." Canadian Adam raises his glass of beer and nods in agreement.

The subject changes and breaks the group up into different pairs. It is at this point that Greg, whom I've only known for a short while, speaks to me about his private life. He has two kids from his Japanese wife, who lives separately from him. They will soon divorce. He had a girlfriend, but she ended the relationship the previous night in order to find a Japanese husband.

He shares this kind of personal information with his students. Those who are close to him know that he will soon divorce. Those who aren't know that he has a girlfriend—he shows photographs of himself in Izu, Shizuoka with her. A friend of a student followed him home, after a dinner date. She followed him into his house, but told him that she isn't easy. They didn't have sex.

"I hear that Japanese women have sex with the man on the third date," he says. "That's what my students tell me."

He speaks of his children, too, and mentions a recent trip to Tokyo Disneyland. An employee allowed a Japanese man and his daughter onto a certain ride, although she was too big for it, but did not allow Greg to take his son on the ride.

"I no longer kick their feet on the train or snap at them like I used to do," he says. "I have decided that you don't have any control in their country. You have to live with the unfair treatment."

What you can learn about a man over a beer. He must be very lonely at thirty-two. Although he doesn't know it, he teaches me the importance of discretion. Students come to the school to learn English, not to hear about a teacher's private troubles. We aren't in the classroom to talk about ourselves. Students use that kind of data against him, on their evaluations, one stated that Greg complained about his marriage and financial problems. Another said that he talked too much about himself. A third refused to take his class again. But Greg doesn't understand why students react that way. He doesn't find anything unusual about blending his private and public lives.

Canadian Adam asks me in front of the group whether I had many girlfriends. I tell him that I only have one.

5

A standard workday involves coming in at half past noon. You clock in, check your schedule, pull your files, plan lessons, and start teaching at 1:15. You have four successive fifty-minute classes with five-minute breaks in between each, before taking lunch for an hour. After that, you teach five more classes. Then, you punch out and go home. A hard schedule, but you get used to it.

Today, I had a bunch of housewives, some university students, and some businesspeople. One housewife in particular sticks in mind because of her idea of a vacation. She's recently been to Italy for five days. The flight to Milan from Tokyo took about thirteen hours. She had three full days to go sightseeing (a day in Milan, a day in Venice, a day in Rome), as she battled jet lag. She returned to Tokyo from Milan on the final day. She tells everyone willing to listen about the splendid time she had. I later learn that kind of extreme travel is common among Japanese businesspeople.

Another memorable one prefers to study biographical articles about Elvis Presley, rather than our textbook's grammar lesson. No one wants to teach him. He's a beginner who requests advance material. He has a reputation for screaming and punching the walls. He is flatulent. He once said that he wanted to kill all Canadian teachers, and called a few of them "pigs." He gets away with his antics because he's rich. He always buys a lot of private classes, the most expensive on offer. As long as he helps the sales staff reach their quotas, they will ignore anything short of physical assault. So, today, they give him to me.

Thank God he behaves, without any anti-North American sentiment or farting. Afterwards, three teachers rush into my cubicle to make sure everything's all right.


6


Greg says his girlfriend broke up with him for good a few days ago. She told him that she used him. She lived with him for a year without paying any rent and managed to save three million yen. Now, she plans to go to Ireland to marry a man she dated a little over a year ago. The Irish guy has recently visited her. "That's why she was away for a week," Greg says. "I thought she went to visit her parents."

She also attributed their breakup to what she described as his drinking problem and inability to speak Japanese. Those statements really hurt Greg. He claims that as of this weekend, he has stopped smoking and drinking and that he now plans to study Japanese more rigorously. Don't tell Greg about your friend from childhood who's become a professor of engineering at an American university, and with who, until recently, you haven't been in contact for ten years, because your co-worker will reveal his insecurities about teaching English conversation to speakers of Japanese.

"Did you tell him what you do?" he asks. "Of course."

"You must be close."

You must be close. In other words, why else would an American university engineering prof hang around an English-conversation teacher? There is a myth that anyone from an English-speaking country, regardless of their educational credentials, can teach his mother tongue. Another myth is that all you have to do is look handsome, smile, and laugh a lot. Then, there's the image that English teachers abroad are simply tourists who choose to stay longer. Greg's self-esteem is flagging, so of course he caves into these misconceptions and ends up feeling, like many teachers, underappreciated, disrespected, undervalued, and even inferior to other professionals.

I don't take it personally. Truth be told, I used to believe those myths. Yet, the value of English-conversation teachers increases in places where there is a shortage, and it is an honorable way to make a living abroad. American English-language teachers in Japan receive their salaries in Japanese yen. Taking the exchange rate between yen and U.S. dollars into consideration, we earn almost double the salary of U.S. teachers. Expatriate workers, at the time of this writing, are allowed by law to earn almost $80,000, without having to pay any U.S. taxes, though we do have to file. In Japan, full-time workers pay a tax rate of

20 percent, while part-time workers pay 10 percent. My friends back home complain about having to pay almost 40 percent of their salaries in local, state, and federal taxes.

I have met "mere" English-conversation teachers in Tokyo who are putting their children through international schools here, with the help of their spouse's income; buying property in the United States, self-funding graduate school, traveling every year; and in short, enjoying a quality of life here that would be unheard of on the same salary in their home countries.

Make no mistake; there are teachers who struggle to get by just like everyone else, but for the ambitious ones, for those who have a well-defined plan and are willing to scale down their standard of living, much more can be saved here in a shorter period of time than in New York City.

Another advantage is that you're suddenly made time rich. A full-time contract in my current position is twenty-five working hours a week. With the extra time, you can do whatever suits you: develop hobbies, work second and third jobs for more savings, or sleep longer. I've seen more of the world from Tokyo than I would have working in the U.S., where workers get two weeks of vacation a year. Japanese national holidays bring the total of paid vacation days to about four weeks. Most teachers travel abroad to a country other than their own at least once a year. That's more than can be said for the average American foreign-language teacher at home, where the percentage of U.S. passport holders is frighteningly low. According to figures from the State Department, about 12 percent of the American population have passports.

Most white-collar workers in the United States suffer from a kind of time famine. According to a report on global labor trends by the International Labour Organization, U.S. workers work the longest hours on the job among industrialized nations. With those increasing hours come increased stress, because there is always more to do and fewer hours to do it in. My American friends are always complaining that they are "ridiculously busy." Tolerance for stress is a kind of status symbol there. The more stress, the more important your position is within the company, or so they want you to believe. But I no longer buy it. "I'm writing a draft and a brief almost simultaneously," wrote one acquaintance. And for what? The loyalty they show their companies doesn't exactly guarantee their employment. Indeed, uncertainty during the cycle of economic recession partly explains the longer hours and higher stress.

Having worked in stressful environments, I find it refreshing to focus solely on my own duties, without penalty. Conversation teachers work alone, not in a group. Thus, they can avoid group politics and petty gossip and simply do their jobs. They don't even have to socialize with anyone after work or attend any company parties during the year. In many other professions, building and developing relationships is as much a part of the job as finishing your work. Among English teachers at stable conversation schools in Japan, however, the unwritten rule is that if you fulfill your responsibilities, you will receive the paperwork for another one- to three-year visa. Some of my colleagues have been with the company for ten years or more. We would have to try really hard to lose our jobs—for instance, I would have to create problems by dating or trying to date students, miss class often, fall asleep in class, or receive many complaints about poor preparation or a poor attitude.

A final perk is that teachers are respected in Japan. Here, it's a respectable occupation, teaching. We are seen here as worldly, cosmopolitan, and sophisticated. Counterparts in New York City paint a bleak picture of the salary, social status, and working conditions. Many teachers at home also have to deal with critical classroom management problems. Poorly funded school districts have periodic situations in which the police have to get involved. Part of the reason for this is because the value of similar teachers decreases when there is a surplus, as in the U.S., where the English language isn't the commodity that it is in Japan.

The business of teaching foreign languages at a competitive school is recession proof. When there are fewer jobs elsewhere, more students study English to gain a competitive edge. In the context of a worldwide recession, resulting in a high percentage of lost jobs among white collar workers, expatriate teachers in Tokyo have a really good thing.

But, surprisingly, some teachers don't know a good thing when they experience it. You wouldn't believe the kind of whining that goes on at the company. Some teachers complain about having to work on Saturdays, about having too many—repeat, too many—consecutive classes, without a longer break. One teacher today says that "Sitting in the rain by myself is better than teaching." And, "Beating myself is a lot better than teaching." And who is he? A part-timer who has been unsuccessful at getting more scheduled teaching hours, and who is feeling pressure for money now that his wife is a few months pregnant. Unsatisfied staff should (1) quit their jobs, and (2) try finding a newer position in their own countries with the same benefits and salary. Only then will they swiftly realize that they will have to work longer and harder at home in a more emotionally volatile environment for less money. Once they see the error of their thinking, they'd come flying back to Tokyo for more of what they used to have.

Given a well-thought-out plan, as well as some well-thought-out money, an American teacher's transition home to the U.S. will be much easier than returning on the hopes of finding something better.

7

The confidence that comes with a regular paycheck makes me more social after work and on my days off. I read about a Ghanaian independence day party in the weekly English-language publication and decided to expose myself more to all that Tokyo has to offer. I already know what it's like to remain isolated at home, wasting the day away.

The celebration attracts more black people in one setting than I had ever seen in Japan. I thought that I had reentered Harlem. Black African women sport colorful dresses and cloth of different colors wrapped around their heads. Black men pose with hands crossed in their two-piece suits. Some wear jeans and conservative shoes. Our shared experience of foreignness in Japan and our similar complexions are comforting.

Several tables of ethnic food decorate the back of the huge conference room. I opt for a grape soda because the separate entrees of beans, meat, and vegetables don't look appetizing. My opinion, however, is in the minority. At a nearby table, a white woman dressed in African attire is guttling the food as if it were a sort of last supper.

Quite a few Ghanaian men arrive with local women on their arms. A medium-complexioned baby sits in his Japanese mother's lap; he looks about two years old. The sight of intercultural relations is natural in this environment. One Japanese women standing alone near the table of sodas works as a photographer, and has just returned from Kenya and Ghana, where she photographed African village life. She doesn't have an exhibition, but offers to meet in the future to show me some of her work.

"My boyfriend is not the jealous type," she says, pointing to a bulky African man dressed in a gray suit. He doesn't smile.

We discuss foreign-language study and some of the circumstances that brought me to Japan, until a commotion on the other end of the room distracts us. About thirty chairs line each side of the room. In the middle space, a slim, gray-haired man, clad in kente cloth and brown sandals, moves his body femininely to the beat of bass and drums, while people cheer him on. Then, a healthy-shaped woman, with round buttocks that pushes up her dress, makes her way to the floor, moving her shoulders and elbows as if she will, at any moment, fly off into the sunset. Someone lets out a high-pitched scream, and about two dozen people join the dancing, while everyone else watches.

Japanese officials and their wives sit on one side of the room, closest to the dancing, with expressionless faces. Their reserve suggests that they are here only as a gesture of respect to the African ambassadors to Japan.

After the festivities, as I walk toward the train station on a dark and secluded road, a blue car pulls up besides me. The African guy in the driver's seat says that he also attended the function and asks me whether I need a ride. As he drives, we have a pleasant, easy conversation. The subject of women enters the discussion. He tells me that marrying a Japanese woman enabled him to stay in Japan.

"That's the only way to do it," he says.

I understand what he means. Finding work during a recession

can be hard, especially without proper credentials, connections, and experience. But I'm not making any excuses. My bout with poverty has left me vehemently opposed to looking like a man who avoids work and lives off women.

## 8

I renew old friendships to find out whether I've been missing anything. At a Thai restaurant in the Ebisu section of Tokyo, I ask Marie if she thinks about returning to Paris, and the twenty-four-year-old French jewelry buyer says pointedly that she misses neither France nor her own family.

"How can I miss home when we moved every four years because of my father's work?" Marie's father works at a home for under-privileged children. She holds a grudge against him for shifting his attention to the other kids under his responsibility, and for their peripatetic existence. "Each time I made friends, I had to eventually leave the city," she says, looking into her gin tonic.

Her childhood situation accounts for why she isolates her-self here. Although she speaks Japanese, most of her friends are French, including her best friend and flat mate, who despises Japanese people so much she is looking for work in Hong Kong. It will only be a matter of time before Marie does the same thing. Were it not for our ties in Paris as students, we would have little to talk about.

Still, hers is a point of view that I share. Return to what? You spend a few days catching up on people's lives. Then, you want to leave because you feel so lonely. Few friends. You have nev-er learned how to be a friend, because you were often alone by choice and too ashamed of your circumstances to invite people home like most children do. You don't learn strong interpersonal skills. Those acquaintances you do have prefer not to speak about your overseas experiences for more than thirty minutes. And who wants to confront all that pain? No dental insurance. No medical insurance. No life insurance. People strapped for cash, feeling the sting of joblessness or underemployment. You want to help, but don't want to get pulled down into the barrel. Even if you give one million dollars, you feel that some people will be in the same position a year later.

Only Claude, Marie's Belgian friend, says that he misses his home. He misses the ritual of eating at a certain cafe each Sunday. At midnight, he rings to invite me to a "black music party" in Shibaura. I wonder why he didn't mention it in front of Marie.


# 9


"The problem with my girlfriend is that she's too independent and too opinionated," Claude tells me over linguine at Cappriciosa's in Roppongi, shaking his head. Furthermore, his Japanese girlfriend hasn't spent any time with him recently because of her alleged workload at school and her responsibilities at home. She does all the cooking because her mother was recently in an accident. "'We can love each other and share our love over the phone, too,'" she told Claude last week.

"And my first Japanese girlfriend was the exact opposite," he says. "I had to make all the decisions; she had no opinion on anything."

A few months ago, the couple gave no indication of their problems at the Lollipop Bar in Akasaka Mitsuke. They appeared as happy as newlyweds. According to Claude, it was a façade. "Our disagreements usually arise when we are alone."

His girlfriend recently spent some time with her Japanese ex-boyfriend while he was in Tokyo on business. Afterward, she told Claude that she was confused.

"I didn't know what that meant," he says.

Try sayonara.

## 10

We are among the first one hundred men to enter the dance club free. The dimly lit, sparely decorated place has a lot of space, but few people. Video screens connected to gadgets hanging from the ceiling show dated episodes of rap music videos. A Caucasian man stands near a Japanese woman sitting on a stool near the bar. The distance and lack of conversation between them make it difficult to determine whether they are friends or not. Two bulky black men in business suits walk side-by-side around the area, eyeing the small group of people present. Based on how they are inspecting the place, I suspect that they helped organize the evening.

A black male wearing a fez strolls into the club alone. His red, black, and green leather jacket has the number eight stitched in the back. The hat, jacket, baggy jeans, and high-top white sneakers give him hoodlum appeal.

Claude and I order drinks from the bar. When I turn around toward the dance floor, I see the man in the fez dancing with two Japanese women in high-heeled pumps and black sequined miniskirts. No one else dances until the second hour.

A group of young Japanese women wanders into the club. The eyes of one widen upon seeing a familiar person, one of the bulky men in a suit. She jumps on him and locks her legs around his waist. They talk about past meetings and mutual acquaintances. Her friends watch and giggle in unison. Here, all the women look the same: slim build, flesh-revealing outfits, permed or cropped hair dyed brownish orange, and tanned skin.

One woman dressed in dark colors dances alone. Compared with the anorexic ones, she is healthy, wide hipped, full breasted, and muscular legged, with long, straight, black hair.

"I don't speak English," she says at the bar, when I ask her to dance.

"That's OK."

The dance floor's intimacy and dim lighting give me the chance to study Reiko. Although her body is voluptuous, she isn't strikingly beautiful. Her teeth are crooked and stained. She has a pointy chin and an under bite. But her clothes are of the highest quality, and reflect what Japanese office ladies in their early twenties consider fashionable. Tight-fitting red top, black miniskirt, suede boots that reach the knee, and a Rolex watch. She says she chooses her outfits the day before. Her wardrobe is more important to her than anything else.

I feel caged. Excluding Claude, who is shadow dancing, we are alone on the floor and everyone is watching. Even the two bulky men in suits eye us from the balcony. I wouldn't be so self-conscious were she not dancing more soulfully than me.

Reiko comes to Tokyo from Fukuoka, Kyushu for her university studies. She works part-time at a museum. Her ambition is to visit the U.S. She speaks some broken English, but introduces me in Japanese to her two friends, a salary man, who by all indications is the only native male here, and a native woman. I decline their offer to join them. Instead, Reiko and I exchange telephone numbers.

Claude now wants to go to a new club in the area. "There's no cover charge for women tonight," he says. From across the street, we watch the doormen, wearing hooded, full-length nylon coats, as they coordinate the crowd of people. Inching toward the door is a queue of tanned women in high heels and skin-tight clothing. As I deliberate over whether to check it out, we see a couple exit from a white concrete building nearest us. It's the fellow in the fez. He's walking toward the first club with a shorter Japanese woman, hand in hand.

"He was in there waxin' and taxin," says a young black male who's sitting on the sidewalk, against the building, with two white friends. "Waxin' and taxin."

The fez guy turns halfway around, and says in a thick baritone, "I gotta make my... *contribution* to U.S.–Japan relations. You know what I'm sayin'?"

## 11

Claude and I bid farewell in Roppongi. On my way home, I spot two Japanese police officers, accompanied by a television crew, questioning a foreign woman selling bouquets of artificial flowers and colored lights. The police check if her partner has a license. He doesn't. They force them to leave. The scene wasn't staged for a Japanese television drama; though, it had been planned in advance to embarrass foreign street vendors in Roppongi, Tokyo's district of distractions, and to boost the police's reputation.

I wander in the direction of Tokyo Tower, hoping to find the street vendor who sells flowers at late hours. Across from the Roi building, I see a crowd surrounded by lights and cameras. The same police officers question a Caucasian man selling sparkly shirts and hats.

"You illegal," one police officer says in his broken English.

"I'm going," the man says. "Yes, go now."

The television cameras record the encounter in its entirety. Nearby stands a Japanese man dressed in a black leather jacket. He's holding a long microphone in his right hand. I regret not having my notebook, and the only paper I have is a wad of receipts from my wallet.

The police walk past a Japanese vendor's food truck.

One officer whispers something in his ear. At that point, I rush ahead to see how many foreign vendors are on the block. Past groups of men hastily packing their bags. I see an Iranian man selling jewelry, and warn him about the police and the cameras. He asks his Japanese friend to watch his goods while he investigates. As I return from Roppongi's main intersection, the Iranian guy is running back to his wares.

The police catch a man and question him extensively. As I write, one woman asks me whether I know about the circumstances. Suddenly, someone screams. A Japanese woman in a red dress is yelling at the man in the black leather jacket. She pushes him against a metal gate and kicks him. The filming stops. The performance ends. She isn't part of the script. In the distance, another Japanese woman dressed in a light blue suit is being held on the ground by the police. One member of the crowd says that her knee is bleeding. I notice blood on her white stockings. It isn't clear whether she was pushed down or accidentally knocked down. When the crowd disperses, I ask the street vendor whether the woman was with him, but he says the incident was separate from his harassment.

"I'm still in shock," he says, slowly packing his belongings.

I pass the Iranian man's display of gold-colored jewelry again. He nods with his arms crossed in a gangster's lean. A syncopated drum beat pours out of the speakers near his knee.

I reach the corner closest to Johnny Rocket's hamburger shop. The police are there with the two Japanese women waiting for the light. I walk toward Almond coffee shop for a taxi to a train station further away, but they are all full. I want to get out of this jungle fast. As I return to the sidewalk, I see out of the corner of my eye someone's body jerk behind me. The person approaches. It's the Japanese man in the black leather jacket, still holding the microphone. He's alone.

"You, you gathering information?" he asks in broken English. "You a reporter?"

"Excuse me?" I look downward, as he moves the microphone closer.

We make eye contact. I turn to walk away, but he grabs my right shoulder and spins me around. Not knowing what will happen next, I remove my glasses in case he decides to swing. We stare at each other in silence. He mutters something that sounds like "OK," while backing away. I turn around again and walk ahead, stopping only briefly to write my observations on the margins of receipts.


## 12

Reiko and I are listening to soul music in my room. She says that she works late evenings at a Ginza hostess bar "for extra money, and as a favor to a friend." I thought she worked only at a museum. She now has more respect for hostesses: a lot of Japanese doctors come to the bar, and the hostesses are expected to carry on a conversation with them.

"Often, I study many books, but the words are so hard for me," she says in Japanese. I have always associated hostess bars with only sexual friction. I never knew that doctors frequent expensive bars to discuss their jobs. She smokes a Carleton cigarette near the window, and later watches an American movie on television. In English, she says, "You speak like white."

"What do you mean?"

"When I go to the military base, the black guys always say, 'Yo, yo, yo, Reiko, yo Reiko. But you don't talk like that."

So that's where she learned to dance so soulfully. I wonder how much time she spends on the military base. She tells me she goes to discos and bars just about every weekend, including Sunday, to counter loneliness. Her Japanese boyfriend works in Osaka, a mere three hours away by train, but rarely calls her.

Her assumption that black men in the military are representative of all black men is curious, but expected.

"All blacks don't speak like that," I say. "Just like all Japanese people don't all speak Japanese the same way. Those living in Osaka or Okinawa speak Japanese differently from those living in Tokyo, right? It depends on your educational background, work, your environment..."

"I see."

Sometime later, loud snoring disturbs my sleep. I wake up muzzy-headed, and am horrified to see Reiko at my side. She's sleeping in a wine-colored top and matching underpants. It's three a.m. Oh, God. What have I done to this woman? What has she done to me? What have we been doing? Her bra is on the floor, next to a Japanese lyrics insert from James Brown's "I

Feel Good" CD. Guilt about Reiko's presence keeps me awake until morning.

I'm hardly a religious man, but I have a strange feeling that her existence was some kind of temptation. I am meant to be living a rigid, disciplined work schedule and lifestyle. While Reiko is still sleeping, I go to the closet and retrieve my international edition of the Bible. An old friend's gift just before I came to Japan. His inscription tells me to start with Paul's second letter to Timothy.

But mark this: "There will be terrible times in the last days. People will be lovers of themselves, lovers of money, boastful, proud, abusive, disobedient to their parents, ungrateful, unholy, without love, unforgiving, slanderous, without self-control, brutal, not lovers of the good, treacherous, rash, conceited, lovers of pleasure rather than lovers of God—having a form of godliness but denying its power. Have nothing to do with them."

I'm going to hell. No one should have anything to do with me. I should avoid myself.

Reiko prefers to stay while I am at work, but I urge her to return home. I don't want her examining my belongings. Later, I throw her number in the trash. Although my other priorities are clear, I know I will probably regret it.


## 13

In puritanical fashion, I find salvation through work. Day by day, I work longer hours. Week by week, I gain additional confidence. Month by month, I save more money and waste less time. I even add second and third jobs to my schedule to account for every hour of the week, and to stash away more yen. I sacrifice every indulgence for my financial health.

I try to take the advice of American social critic and novelist Toni Cade Bambara. "Revolution begins with the self, in the self. The individual, the basic revolutionary unit, must be purged of poison and lies that assault the ego and threaten the heart, that hazard the next larger unit—the couple or pair—that jeopardize the still larger unit—the family or cell—that put the entire movement at peril."

After awhile, I can afford to reject extra work. I reach financial security. I pay off my university loans. I improve my quality of life. I work on making a transition from living to work to working to live. Indeed, life is much better. Now all I need is a wife and I will be complete, but I can't forget those days of regular nightmares. I decide to return to the States on vacation for the first time in ages.

Etched in my memory is a scripture from Philippians 4:12. "I know what it is to be in need, and I know what it is to have plenty. I have learned the secret of being content in any and every situation, whether well fed or hungry, whether living in plenty or want. I can do everything through him who gives me strength." Amen.

CHAPTER TEN

## Authenticity

THE SOVIET UNION LIFTED Cosmonaut 3rd Class Sergei
Krikalev into space for what was to be a short exploration in early
1991. Budget, bureaucratic, and territorial problems kept him
stuck in a space station for 310 days. While he orbited Earth, his
homeland fought off a coup, changed its title, its flag, its anthem,
and its state structure. Indeed, he returned to a place different
from the one he left.

Kazakhstan, one of the Commonwealth of Independent States
that has replaced the USSR. His uniform sleeve still bore the letters
"USSR" and the red Soviet flag. But upon his return, Mr. Krikalev
reportedly said that the change "has not been so drastic" because
his homeland is still united, though under a different name.

I stayed away from the United States for five years, during
which I spun in and out of different orbits of Japanese and Western employment in Tokyo. Now, as I prepare for my first trip
home, having made a full financial recovery, it doesn't take a
great leap of the mind to intuit that many changes have taken
place in New York City.

I can't wait. In the pouring rain, I walk slowly up a narrow
Tokyo path. On each side are a few, small, two-story concrete

houses. Some have weeds and plants out front. Most are absent of life. All are close enough for people to hand things to their neighbors through side windows. I search for a taxi at the end. At my left is a vending machine that sells oolong tea, cafe au lait, and C and C lemon, with ten percent fruit juice, for 110 yen. To the right is a photography shop that advertises portraits of Japanese families in traditional garb. Normally, I would walk to Harajuku Station from my place, but the day's weather and my luggage forestall that plan.

The taxi door opens and closes at the touch of a button near the driver's seat. It takes about ten minutes to get to my destination in traffic. By the time I step out of the taxi and into a crowd of blue suits and umbrellas, the rain has changed to a mere drizzle. I ride the Japan Railway Yamanote line to Shinjuku Station, and then rush to tracks three and four for an express train to Narita Airport.

One of the first things I'm going to do at home is eat alone in a restaurant serving Southern cuisine. I look forward to having a meal in a civilized environment. No more worrying about whether someone has contaminated my food, or spat in my drink, as I do in Tokyo—that is, unless it's buffet style. Equally, I won't have to meet the eyes of some customers staring at me like dogs at a dinner table. In the States, I'll socialize and explore Manhattan in total comfort, as a local.

While I suffer through banal in-flight movies and mediocre U.S. sitcoms, I write down telephone numbers of all my friends in Japan. I fear forgetting, as though flying through the International Date Line will somehow delete my memory of all things Japanese. The plane shows one movie that assists my transition back. The theme is about confronting and coming to terms with your past, no matter how painful. In it, two men, one black, the other white, learn that they have the same mother. A married white father raped his black maid; she died while giving birth to a son, and he was raised white. Years later, his adopted mother dies, leaving him a letter that reveals the truth about his beginnings, and urges him to discover his black brother. He survives a series of accidents and embarrassments that ultimately lead the two strangers to an understanding and appreciation of each other.

It's rare to watch this kind of movie on an overwhelmingly Japanese flight. I feel that someone had selected it for me. I'm reminded of my strained relationship with my separated parents and brother. I have been terrible about keeping in touch with anyone from abroad.

The challenge of first-generation university graduates living abroad is to never pretend about their past; they should stay tied to what makes them unique. But it takes effort to love and accept yourself. How easy it is to escape from all familiar experiences when you're existing more than ten time zones away from home. I avoid saying anything that may betray my working class origins—or, as my childhood friends would say, "broke class"—even when it's appropriate to do so. The time I lied to Kumiko comes to mind.

According to biographer Marshall Frady, Reverend Jesse Jackson once said, "You know, people always ask why is Jesse Jackson running for the White House." Jackson is a two-time Democratic presidential candidate. "They never seen the house I'm running from. Three rooms, tin-top roof, no hot or cold running water, slop jar by the bed, bathroom in the backyard in the wintertime. Wood over the windows, wallpaper put up not for decoration but to keep the wind out... Yet, I remain connected to all this. By continuing to live in those experiences here, you have high-octane gas in your tank—keep those experiences flowing through your soul, it gives you authenticity."

Seen from that point of view, my first visit home in five years is an attempt to find humility. Then, and only then, can I relate to people better and live in the world more comfortably.

## 2

A polite driver in a yellow taxi takes me from John F. Kennedy Airport to Manhattan by the Triboro Bridge, at about 10:00 p.m. According to an article in New York magazine, that route is the fastest and cheapest. The driver says that the government has recently established a flat rate of thirty dollars for passengers going into the main borough. Plus tolls, the total fare comes to a few dollars less than the article estimated.

I see my first homeless person just as the car exits from the highway onto 125th Street and Second Avenue. She's an older black woman with a cane, walking slowly in the middle of the street, shaking a cup from left to right, and mumbling to herself.

Through the darkness, I don't notice much, except for the bright neon signs advertising the area's flood of fast food restaurants. There is a Mama's Fried Chicken, a Kennedy's Fried Chicken, and a White Castle hamburger shop on the corner of Frederick Douglass Boulevard. Some things never change.

As the car drives past Fifth Avenue and 125th, the driver locks the doors. I laugh nervously. I ask him whether he thought I was going to run out of the car, but he says he was concerned about the possibility of people entering. I return my tip to my wallet.

He drops me off. I pay the bill, take my luggage from the

backseat, and proceed to the public telephone on the corner. A few people loiter outside of the building, in the darkness. Kids are out and about with nowhere to play but the concrete streets. During a brief chat with my mother, I notice that the yellow cab hasn't departed yet. Why? Hadn't I paid my bill? I thought he was afraid of inner-city people.

I'm hoping he doesn't hound me about the tip, when he gets out of the front seat, walks to the back of the car, and eyeballs me on the phone. If looks could injure, I'd be in critical condition. When I tilt my head for an explanation, he says, "You could have at least closed the door," and slams it shut. The experience floors me. I don't have time to apologize. I really want to explain that from where I came customers need not touch the door; Japanese taxi drivers open and close them with a lever near their steering wheel. I forgot that here it's different. But, before I regain my senses, his tires screech off into traffic.

The building's dinginess hasn't changed. The elevator works, but the light indicating floors doesn't. I have to leap inside because someone baptized the floor, though I don't smell piss. Above the stop button is a sign stating that the inspection certificate is in the main office.

The doors open to a close-up view of my mother with her hair in curlers, arms spread open. Her hair is still black, but time has added weight to her body and rounded her face. I see a different person from before. She takes me on a tour of the new place. She had to move into a smaller apartment once I moved out; a requirement of the rent-controlled residence. I refrain from telling her that the kitchen is the size of my entire room in Tokyo. I feel awkward. Don't quite know what to say after so many years. She calms my nerves by starting with the past.

Daddy entered the hospital for surgery on his leg, Aunt Kitty had a heart attack, her friend Ellen remarried and has a baby, Aunt Hester has joined her on a trip to Atlantic City recently, my brother, six years older, works on 110th Street and Broadway, and my half brother, whom I've never met, or seen pictures of until now, lives in Baltimore with his wife and baby daughter. He works for the post office, dropped out of college, but intends to return. A family man. We look so much like our mother. The same facial features.

She continues. Con Ed (the utilities company, Con Edison) had to come and fix the gas. They were outside doing construction and hit a wrong pipe. The gas and all the lights were out in the building. Had to use an extension cord out in the hall just for my lights, she says. As if that wasn't enough, the ceiling in the bathroom started to leak. When it rains it pours.

She outdoes herself in the kitchen. I haven't had a decent home-cooked meal in years. I'll probably gain a couple of kilos on this trip. Feed me meat. Feed me meat is all I keep saying. Afterwards, we watched a movie about a lawyer connected to the mafia. I'm still unsettled, though, partly due to jetlag, and partly due to not knowing where I'll sleep. There isn't a sofa in the living room. She gave it to my brother and his wife, and there is only a recliner that doesn't recline.

"You don't have to worry about getting a hotel," she says. "I work in the evening from nine until nine in the morning and I'm off on weekends. So you can use the bed at night." I opt for the living room. Feels like I'm on an airplane seat, all over again. But it beats sleeping on a futon, as I do in Tokyo. I don't need a radio. Passing car drivers play their music loud enough for everyone to hear, regardless of the time. Seeping through the windows are the sounds of Ice T, Nas, The Fugees, De La Soul, Keith Sweat, LL Cool J. and Tupac.

So much for peace and quiet. On thinking about how snobbish I've become, I try to rest. Tomorrow, I'll see a movie starring Eddie Murphy, get a physical, and meet some friends.

## 3

What do I find in Manhattan after a five-year absence? The city changed the name of my family's street from Lenox to Malcolm X Boulevard. I have nothing against him, but I prefer the tones of the former name. Prices have increased with inflation. The northern end of Central Park has been revitalized; landscaping gives it a more upscale look than before. The grass is greener, more benches have been added, and the lake is cleaner, and now has algae and ducks.

Condominiums and cooperative apartments have been built on 110th Street, the width of the park. High real estate prices in the city center are attracting to Harlem a solid, middle-class group of professionals who can't afford to buy property elsewhere. The local press anticipate a multiracial Harlem in a generation's time.

There is less crime, more police, and more tourists. Forty-second Street between Broadway and Ninth is a clean place for families. There are large movie theaters and a Warner Brothers shop. It used to be one of the seediest places in the city, the red-light district.

Among the young guardians of popular culture, platinum is in as the jewelry of choice. Gold is out. Cristal champagne is the alcohol with which to be seen—a lot of American pop and rap songs refer to the drink. If you can't afford it, any kind of

Hennessey and Tanqueray will do, but avoid beer if you want to look elite. Clean-shaven heads, as well as braids and afros, are in, which I'm happy about because I'm balding. The wet-haired look is out.

Tattoos are popular. Everyone wants something inked onto their bodies to make a favorable statement about themselves. Look at me, they seem to say, I'm part of a hip, fashionable group. But will they want to have them surgically removed twenty years later? Probably.

I need a tutorial to grasp the creative English-language usages, which are forever changing. At this moment of writing, instead of asking do you understand, some people in my community ask, "Are you feeling me?" Instead of saying I'd rather not talk about it, people say "I don't want to go there." Instead of saying I want to meet some women, some men would say, "I wanna meet some hookers." Or rather than ask how are the women in Tokyo, they'd ask, "How the bitches over there?"

Instead of saying I want to teach you something, they'd say that they "wanna break you off somethin'." You can't describe anything as great or exciting. You have to say that it's "bananas," "retarded," or just "gangsta." You're never nervous; you're "shook." You're not embarrassed; you're "assed out."

My friend becomes my "dog." A woman doesn't playfully hit her female friend. She "bitch slaps" her. She doesn't say that her friend likes to date two men simultaneously. She says that she's "all hoed out."

Money is referred to as "cheese." You don't say that you have a nice or new car. You have a new "whip." When I ask one guy whether he plans to relocate from his apartment into a house, he tells me, yes, he has plans to "make some power moves."

In many ways, I feel like I'm on a different planet. What is worse is that some black people still regard any kind of intellectual pursuit as something to avoid. The American view of black males is so dramatically low right now that people deem the simple act of reading a book as something extraordinary. I'm sitting inside a coffee shop in the Times Square section of Manhattan, fingering through one of the novels I just bought. The colorful Barnes & Noble bag is lying on the table. A black male dressed in business clothes approaches to say how good it is to see a brother reading a book and making purchases at a bookstore.

He means it as a compliment. He says that countering black stereotypes is good, and he is right. But it's not as if I'm reading a Japanese-language text, which would understandably be rare and surprising. I'm insulted, though I don't voice it.

## 4

In *The New Class Society: Goodbye American Dream?* Robert Perruci and Earl Wysong argue that a large part of U.S. society has become more economically vulnerable since the mid-1970s. Twenty percent of Americans are privileged with job security and high wages, while the other eighty are part of a fresh group that lacks the same security and wages.

A visit to the old neighborhood presents a range of working class stories. You hear the obligatory ones about people jailed, killed, or working as blue-collar staff. You hear ones about drug addiction, teenage pregnancies, and dropping out of high school. There are stories of old acquaintances now working in the entertainment industry as rappers and actors. There are stories of university graduates who've fled urban living and entered the middle class. There are stories about families keeping to themselves, working hard, and raising their children, just as in any other cosmopolitan city around the world.

Middle-class, college-educated friends struggle to maintain or to find jobs. One lawyer says that his firm overworked him and that all his hours weren't "billable." He sometimes worked on weekends, and spent less time with his family. "It was killing me," he says. He finally used the services of a professional recruiter to switch from law to the banking sector, where he's now happier and has more time with his wife and child.

A musician friend raves about securing a role in a Broadway production because of the steady work and security on offer. "It's rare," he says, "to know that you have a paycheck for two years."

A consultant and part-time landlord wants to win a local election because then he'll know that "for three years I won't have to worry about a job."

Jonathan Mahler contends that the common theme of the U.S. recession in the new millennium is that not even the most prestigious advanced degrees and the finest business connections are enough to protect white-collar workers from losing their jobs. According to his article, "The New Unemployed," the economic downturn in New York City is worse than the already bleak situation nationwide. Between December 2000 and January 2003, for example, the computer industry cut forty-one percent of its positions. During that same period, the media and communications sector has cut fifteen percent, advertising twenty-five, telecommunications twenty-seven, and Wall Street eighteen percent. In tandem with those job cuts came a sharp drop in self-esteem. Joblessness has forced a lot of middle-aged, married, white males with children to "surrender an idea of who they are or what others thought they were."

He centers the essay around the experiences of three men—two in their fifties, one in his early forties—and on the psychological, emotional, and financial effects of prolonged unemployment. Each had a high-paying, executive position. Each defined himself by his rung on the ladder. Each failed to find similar work after more than a year's time and eventually had to accept or consider taking jobs in other fields at a fraction of their previous salaries. One went from working as an executive vice president of a company in the computer industry to working as a clerk at The Gap. The only reason he accepted the job is because his wife gave him an ultimatum to contribute to the rent or move out. The other two men were warming to the idea of working as teachers in the public school system.

I feel very lucky to have a job and to have a sense of job security. I know what it's like to lose work. I know what it's like to deal with humiliating circumstances and bouts of self-doubt. I know what it's like to have to shed pretensions and to redefine oneself and goals.

5

There are a lot of myths in the inner city. One is that there is a black neighborhood that operates like an extended family. Orlando Patterson blows that story right out of the water in his book, *Rituals of Blood: Consequences of Slavery in Two American Centuries*. The Harvard University sociologist writes that "Afro-Americans are today the loneliest of all Americans." He supports his claim with findings from a 1990 census and two national survey databases. His research shows that the marriage rates of blacks are the lowest in the U.S., their divorce rates are among the highest, most spend most of their lives alone, and that they have fewer supportive friends than most other Americans.

But don't tell that to anyone where you were raised; they believe that "it's all good in the 'hood." Yet, no one cares about you and your life abroad, really, unless caring can persuade you to give them some gift money, buy them something, or do them some kind of favor. Otherwise, you can take those overseas photographs and "shove them up your ass" because they "got bills to pay." That's what their words, actions, and silence sometimes communicate.

Periodic trips home shock the mind, after living in Japan for many years. New York is so segregated by race and class that it's an aberration to have friends or acquaintances from other English-speaking countries. Race is so dominant an issue that everyone looks at life in narrow racial terms, and has an allergy toward a broader perspective.

"Ah, you ain't assimilatin' that much, you're a black man in Tokyo," says a friend from childhood who should have known better. "Is it true they eat dog over there?"

He has it backwards. I hadn't meant that I could somehow transform my physical characteristics into Japanese ones. I meant adapting to Japanese customs and habits, as it's defined in the *Longman Dictionary of Contemporary English*: "to make or become like the people of a country, race, or other group, esp. in ways of behaving or thinking." The bizarre tendency of most Americans, black and white, even those with the best of intentions, is to place limits on how black people should live and view themselves. They use whiteness equally as the only point of reference for a black self-image.

When I first unveiled my Japanese ambitions in 1991, I met a fanfare of rebuke and ridicule. The common litany stated that black men of my generation—those born around 1967—were earmarked for work in Europe or Africa, not Asia, and especially not Japan. Unless, of course, they wanted to end up in a straitjacket somewhere. Most people tried to place limits on my aspirations. Although they believed they were just giving some cautious advice, they were still never at a loss for reasons not to go.

Their main argument was Japan's racist nature, as demonstrated by the comments of politicians there. In 1986, former prime minister Yasuhiro Nakasone, who has driven the nation toward internationalism more than any other elected official, said that the overall intelligence and knowledge of Americans was lowered by the presence of African-Americans, Puerto Ricans, and Mexicans. Two years later, Michio Watanabe of the Liberal Democratic Party voiced that American blacks were comfortable going bankrupt. Two years after that, in 1990, Seiroku Kajiyama, a former justice minister, compared blacks to prostitutes, stating that both destroyed neighborhoods after they moved in.

Contrary to popular opinion, I have found that Japanese people in my generation are very open to English-speakers. But to avoid the risk of sounding naive, let me say that it's true that Japanese locals place foreign races and nationalities on a hierarchy. Nationals from English-speaking countries are higher than those from other Southeast Asian ones. Regarding the country's idea of beauty, the lighter skins are at the top. "There is still a strong demand for child models with Caucasian blood," said a representative of an established, Tokyo-based agency for child models, in a feature story that appeared in an English-language, Japanese-owned newspaper. "The price is highest for blond, blue-eyed kids simply because there are a limited number of them in Japan."

It's true that locals, just like everyone else in the world, have views of black males as dangerous, due to high crime rates, high HIV-infection rates, and high unemployment rates. Less than stellar black depictions in film, literature and on TV certainly don't help. Japanese will examine you closely to see whether you validate those impressions or not. Some will reject you outright, assuming the worst.

It's true that negative racial perceptions among Japanese might cause a plainclothes security officer to follow you in a department store, might prompt a woman to hold her purse tighter, might result in the occasional inferior service at a restaurant, and might make it harder to buy a home. Those kinds of reactions, however, happen sometimes to all foreigners in Japan and to even local Japanese. All one has to do is read local English-language newspapers.

Yet, if you have the educational background, the connections, and a job with a competitive salary that allows you to enjoy a range of leisure activities—and you're friendly and treat people with respect and kindness—you'll be insulated from the worst assumptions about your race and class. Tokyo is as exciting and fun as any other large, cosmopolitan city. Racial concerns certainly won't prevent you from making money and enjoying cultural offerings—unless you let them. If you're not college-educated, lack social contacts, and have a low-paying job on a low rung of the corporate ladder—and you're unfriendly and rude—you'll have a terrible time in Tokyo. The problem, of course, will have nothing to do with race and all to do with your shortage of credentials, skills, and manners.

There are many ways to see oneself in the world. As a resident in two very distinct cultures, I know that people don't have to restrict their personal ideas to a series of binary oppositions: black and white, rich and poor, liberal and conservative, straight and gay, American and foreign. I'm American working in Tokyo with local Japanese as well as Canadians, Australians, New Zealanders, and English people. Narrowing my philosophy to mere racial distinctions would be laughable and pointless.

When I travel to the most rural parts of northern Japan, on vacation, local children look at my dark complexion and say "American" or "A-me-ri-ka jin" (an American person). They never mention Africa. The most derogatory labels spoken there might be "English teacher," the name of a famous American professional athlete or actor, or simply the word "foreigner." And what's wrong with that? It's a hell of a lot better than being called a nigger, a pimp, poor, or illiterate.

I'm not—repeat, not—arguing that Japan is a kind of utopia for black American professionals. It's not. What I'm saying is that working Americans overseas find that issues of class are more dominant on the job and in leisure than those of race. Who you know, where you receive your degree, how much money you earn, and how much you invest in financial instruments are the kinds of factors used to determine your place on the class scale. What matters most in the workplace are skills; what you can do, qualifications; evidence that you can contribute, and personal qualities; how you execute your abilities and relate to your colleagues and customers.

American intellectual Randall Kennedy lends support to the thought of cultural multiplicity in his book, *Interracial Intimacies*. He writes that "a well-ordered multiracial society ought to allow its members free entry into and exit from racial categories, even if the choices they make clash with traditional understandings of who is 'black,' and who is 'white,' and, even if, despite making such choices in good faith, individuals mislead observers who rely on conventional racial signaling."

Henry Louis Gates, Jr. widens the idea in an essay about W.E.B. Du Bois titled "Both Sides Now" in the *New York Times Book Review*. "One ever feels his two-ness—an American, a Negro," Du Bois wrote, in his classic *The Souls of Black Folks*. "Two souls, two thoughts, two unreconciled strivings; two warring ideals in one dark body, whose dogged strength alone keeps it from being torn asunder." Gates, the W.E.B. Du Bois Professor of the Humanities and chair of the Afro-American Studies Department at Harvard University, writes in response that "the only complaint we moderns have is that Du Bois was too cautious in his accounting ... Just two, Dr. Du Bois? Keep counting."

What's necessary for black people interested in living, studying, and working abroad, in general, and in Japan, specifically, is to rid themselves of a slave's mentality that robs them of confidence and restricts their lives. They should free themselves from any assumptions that they can't live fully and happily, internationally, based on their own merits. The last plantation, wrote Debra J. Dickerson, is in the mind. This is how she described the condition of being black and simultaneously American in her book *The End of Blackness*.

"Harry Houdini once famously struggled for hours picking a jail cell lock, only to lean against it in exhaustion and have the door swing open. It had never been locked at all. All that confined him was in his own head."

She's right.

6

The adage "when in Rome, do as the Romans do" rings true in Japan, regardless of one's race, gender, educational, political, or religious background. Tokyo residents absorb a lot of cultural differences into their own lives and routines. Japanese people remove their shoes before entering homes, they shower before entering a bath, they generally eat more rice and fish than red meat—but not dog, which is eaten in South Korea—they separate their trash into burnable and non-burnable bags, and they don't tip at restaurants because a service charge is included in the final bill.

The locals exchange gifts at every chance. If you travel domestically or abroad, on vacation, you bring back a box of goodies for your coworkers and friends to eat. You should also buy gifts if you attend sporting events or visit theme parks. In winter and summer, the nation exchanges seasonal gifts. When you relocate to a new apartment building, you give gifts to everyone on your floor, as a sign that you're a good neighbor and want to blend well into the community. If you visit someone's home, you should bring a gift. Indeed, were gift giving an Olympic sport, Japan would probably win gold.

A reason for the incessant exchange of gifts in Japan is to keep harmony and maintain good relations. An inversion of that kind of etiquette is in David Flusfeder's novel *The Gift*. One character is an unending gift giver. The protagonist, who is unable to compete with him financially, hates him for it. He feels both indebted to the giver and obsessed with outdoing his friend with bigger and better gifts. They each try to out give the other, until, near the end of the book, the poorer friend feels "victimized with benevolence, persecuted with love, and diminished with kindness."

Japanese live according to a string of annual events. An abridged version would show that the first few days of January is a time for family. There is a set menu of traditional food for each day. There are trips to shrines to pray for a better year. In mid-January, there is coming-of-age day on which all twenty year olds attend formal, nationwide ceremonies congratulating them on becoming legal adults. They can now drink and smoke and do all the things their parents do. In February, women give chocolate to men on Valentine's Day. In March, men return the favor on White Day.

A New York City bus driver, who spent three years in the U.S. military, in Yokosuka, Japan, says on his Manhattan route that he misses the motherly treatment of the women. "They would prepare my bath, fix the dinner, wash the clothes, all that," he says. "It's a lot different here."

He's right. The United States has the highest percentage of women in administrative and managerial economic-decision making positions among G8 nations, based on a United Nations report ("The World's Women 2000: Trends and Statistics") that surveys the status of women worldwide. Japan's share, on the other hand, is the lowest of the lot, on par with Tunisia and Cameroon. In April, the start of the business year, cherry blossom viewing parties are in full swing across Japan. They're another excuse to sit underneath a tree with friends and co-workers and to drink alcohol. Not that locals need additional reasons to get drunk.

In May, the nation has a week-long national holiday called Golden Week. In the summer months, gifts of fruit and beer are exchanged to combat the heat. In December, young couples spend the evening at hotels on Christmas Eve. Everyone works on Christmas, a regular business day, apart from the obligatory chicken meal and strawberry shortcake dessert, with one's significant other or spouse in the evening. At year's end, people clean their own homes as if they're about to go on sale, in order to start off the new year correctly.

The same range of crime found in every industrialized country, as well as some psychologically extreme kinds of law breaking, exists in Japan. You have to protect yourself against burglary and car, motorcycle, and bicycle theft. Women have to guard themselves against perverts, especially on trains and buses. But you don't worry about bullet-related crime because Japanese law bans guns.

All Americans—at the moment, only about twelve percent of the entire U.S. population have passports, according to the State Department—can benefit from a stint overseas for work or study. Then, many won't have an intellectual aversion toward most foreign ideas; and they will view themselves in terms of their nationality. Ideally, they'll know better how the world views them.

7

The excitement of home wears off. Sure, it's great to spend time with my mother again, to relax in my childhood environment, to contact relatives and old friends. It's fun to visit favorite restaurants, shop, and watch a lot of movies that will take months to premiere in Asia.

But after about ten days I'm ready to get back to my independent routine. I'm tired of sleeping on the recliner in the living room, my mother's offer of the bed notwithstanding. I have no privacy. No social life. I'm tired of being asked for money. I try to help people out a little, yet five days later, the same adults ask for more loans, which I know they can't pay back. I have to tell them that I'm not a bank.

American legal scholar Stephen Carter, in his book, *Integrity*, writes that "family should be a place of refuge, a place of emotional and spiritual safety in a frustrating and unfriendly or even hostile world. To make the family even an emotionally unsafe place ... will never be an act of integrity; it will almost always be an act of selfishness."

I want to relax during my rare visits home in a calm and tranquil environment, without having to feel that acts of kindness are preludes to inquiries for money. "Do you have X dollars you can spare?" I would love to go home once—just once—and not have to enter any discussions whatsoever about cash: the lack of, the need for, the possibility of having some. I can't spend money on people because they'll think that they can use me. They'll read my kindness as weakness. They'll regard my visits home as a potential payday. And when I'm in need, who can I call? Who can I run to for assistance? Who's got my back? I'd like to see that person. Show me that person. All the sweet talk and promises in the world won't pay the rent. I'm on my own. That partly explains why remaining in Tokyo broke is much easier than returning home broke: You can manage to get help in Japan.

I realize during my visit home that it's difficult to blend my two completely different existences. The gap between my working-class and middle-class friends leaves me uneasy. My interests, hobbies, and even the way I speak cut me off from my class and fill me with guilt. In order to fit into one particular group, I have to break verbs, drink a lot of alcohol, swap stories about

womanizing, curse, wear flashy outfits, display predatory emotions, and eat mostly fast food.

For a different group, I have to talk about how successful
I've become in terms of money earned, things bought, and
fringe benefits, as well as any potential real estate purchases.
That's all they seem to talk about. I have to wear the latest
fashions and accessories as seen in men's style magazines. At
the same time, I have to spend a lot of money socializing at
New York City restaurants.

Both groups are composed only of black people and point to
a divide of middle and working classes. They exist on opposite
ends of a spectrum. In between, there are many other circles of
acquaintances with their own unique culture and mores. But I
no longer care about advertising my success, as people so often
do in capitalist societies. The experience of cash-strapped circumstances abroad has transformed how I live. I prefer to wear my
recent financial gains lightly. Money talk, unless it's something
about the foreign exchange rate, is an unsuitable topic of conversation with both family and friends.

Abroad, I always speak about what Manhattan has to offer. Everything is described in superlatives: the best this, most delicious
that, the oldest whatever. Those tales, however, need to be taken
with a grain of salt.

Staff can be incompetent and rude. One waiter adds the total
incorrectly and becomes annoyed when I bring the mistake to his
attention. So much for a simple apology to the customer.

I wish to have a photograph repaired. The staff say to pick it
up in three days, but when I come back three days later, it isn't
ready. They can't tell me why and fail to produce what I paid
for in advance.

I stop by a post office to cash a money order. The older woman clerk wants to know my age, after returning my passport. "What's someone like you doing in Tokyo?" When I redirect the conversation to the money order, she tells me that she should have looked at my identification for my age. She's smiling. Yet, I leave wondering whether they pay staff to treat customers—well, so familiar.

I visit the Schomberg Library in Harlem. The idea is to relax in the oasis of black letters. A black security guard not only eyes my every move, but peeks—repeat, peeks—over my shoulder a few times to see what I'm reading. *Do I have a magnet in my spine?* I ask myself. At one point, he literally stands behind me. So much for discretion.

I criticize him. He summons his boss, an older dark-skinned man with gray hair and glasses who tells me that some people try to steal books and periodicals. So they have to be extra cautious.

But I'm sitting here at a desk in the widest open reading space.

"No disrespect intended," he says.

Staff keep their distance afterwards.

I spend an afternoon downtown shopping for clothes. I'm carrying two bags in each hand when I notice seven young black males dressed in baggy, oversized outfits that give them thug airs. They are looking directly at me from the next corner. Instead of passing them on the way to the subway, as planned, I step into the street and hail a taxi quickly. On the way home, I recognize that I could have been misreading the situation. But I sure did not feel good or safe in the moment.

I enter a soul-food restaurant alone in Harlem and order smothered chicken and side orders of macaroni and cheese and candied yams. Halfway through the meal, a group of six black adults sit beside my table. "I can't believe you're jealous of someone else's food," says a woman in the group to one of the men, as they wait for their order. "Don't worry about him."

I ignore them. I don't even make eye contact. But I do know that I'm "him." I can't believe it, either. We're supposed to be brothers and sisters, right? I'm here in the heart of Harlem, surrounded and served by black people, in a black-owned restaurant, and I have to listen to meal-spoiling comments.

My people, Americans in general, and African-Americans in particular, can be infuriating, just like everyone else in the world. I turn on the radio inside my mother's apartment, pour myself a glass of iced tea, and exhale in the recliner. I think that I'll be a little more tolerant when I return to Tokyo.

CHAPTER ELEVEN

# Coda

*Oh, you are young, you are young–be glad of it: be glad of it and live. Live all you can: it's a mistake not to. It doesn't so much matter what you do–but live. This place makes it all come over me. I see it now. I haven't done so–and now I'm old. It's too late. It has gone past me–I've lost it. You have time. You are young. Live!*
*–William Dean Howells, Henry James Letters.*

Sprinting toward a life of health, spirituality, and living, rather than obsessing about trivialities, I find it necessary to review what reduced circumstances in Tokyo have taught me.

## 1. The Price of Wasted Kindness

"Do not spend your strength on women, your vigor on those who ruin kings," states Proverbs 31:3 to male seekers of wisdom. But I needed firsthand knowledge to understand that a pointless life awaits people who devote themselves to immediate gratification and to pleasures of the flesh. The stress here is on the word "devote." Samplings of Japanese erotic love are at the fingertips of all foreign men in Tokyo. You don't exactly have to dedicate yourself to taking full advantage of every single opportunity—potential, actual, and imagined—that comes your way.

Indeed, your very existence depends on how well you do in school, how well you are able to navigate different cultures and interact with others, and how fluent you are in capitalism and in financial planning.

The downside of focusing on the insubstantial aspects of life is vulnerability in times of economic disaster, and a waste of resources on uncaring people. A present-progressive life looks really good, until tomorrow comes and you can't pay bills, can't enjoy a range of leisure activities, and can't maintain healthy relationships.

### 2. The Importance of Not Taking Yourself Seriously

Andrea Lee describes occasions of unwanted attention about which some American newcomers to foreign cities complain, in *Russian Journal,* her memoir on ten months in Moscow and Leningrad, in 1978–79. "It was in the subway that night that I endured the unblinking stare of the Russian populace, a stare already described to me by Tom [her husband] and by friends who had been to the Soviet Union before."

She continues, "'You will never not be stared at,' they told me, advising me to stare back coolly and steadily, especially at the shoes of my tormentors, since the average Soviet shoe is an embarrassment of cracked imitation leather."

I used to feel the same way in Tokyo about Japanese people's interest until I realized how unconnected their glances are to my life and how much wasted energy goes into thinking about the situation. Locals make aliens the object of their stares, photographs, and comments, in addition to their frustrations, pressures, and sporadic moments of jealousy. Who cares?

That's the case wherever there are outsiders. Yet, it's important to not take yourself too seriously when abroad. Learn to
laugh at the perceptions Japanese people have of different nationalities and races.

The healthiest way to handle the inevitable spotlight is too not
worry—unless your civil liberties, work, or property is at stake. Con-
centrate instead on more important aspects of life and let other
people squander their time on matters beyond their control.

### 3. The Error of Defining Success by Work and Possessions

The problem with defining success by employment and status,
possessions and accommodations, is that the happiness of having them wears off quickly, and you suddenly feel defeated the
moment you lose them.

The emphasis we place on getting rich in order to impress others and to become a member of the elite should be transferred
to time with family, concerns about our overall health, and the
pursuit of hobbies we enjoy. Most people lack time to relish life,
even though they are rich enough to worry about things other
than money and the trappings of wealth.

### 4. The Limits of Race

"So, what's it like being a black man in Tokyo?" asked an African-
American woman of intelligence, wit, and grace, in a restaurant
in downtown Cairo, Egypt.

Perhaps she had read an article from the Tokyo press that used
the Japanese environment of child models to describe for its English-language readership the country's ultimate idea of beauty.

A better question, though, would have been what's it like being male, or being a college-educated, middle-class, American

male, in Japan. Or else, simply, what's it like? Drop the black part. Matters of race never play any role in my daily decisions, habits and routines. They don't determine where I work, exercise, shop, eat, travel, live, and socialize. Nor do they affect who I date and befriend.

Issues of class, on the other hand, are the most relevant. Money and free time dominate experiences in Tokyo. As a city, it was rated as the worlds most expensive during most of the 1990s, in an annual survey conducted by The Economist Intelligence Unit.

I wrote it earlier and mean it even more now, if you have the educational background, the connections, and the job, and you're friendly and treat people with respect and kindness, you'll be insulated from the directness of any possible unpleasant aspects of race and class. Tokyo, at the same time, will be as exciting and fun as any other large, cosmopolitan city in the world.

From that standpoint, racial concerns will never have a major impact on your Japanese thoughts—they certainly won't prevent you from making money and enjoying cultural offerings. What's necessary for black people who live, study and work in Japan, in particular, and in any foreign city, in general, is to rid themselves of a slave's mentality that robs them of confidence and restricts their lives. They should free themselves from any assumptions that they can't live fully and happily, internationally, based on their own merits.

Here's another passage worth repeating: "The last plantation," wrote Debra J. Dickerson, "is in the mind." This is how she described the condition of being black and simultaneously American in her book *The End of Blackness*.

"Harry Houdini once famously struggled for hours picking a jail cell lock, only to lean against it in exhaustion and have the door swing open. It had never been locked at all. All that confined him was in his own head."

She's right.


### 5. The Benefits of Reinventing Yourself

Learning new skills will help you to remain competitive in the workplace. Life's priorities change whenever there is fear of unemployment, underemployment, restructuring, or unexpected events, and simply when you change your mind about what you want out of life. If you can adapt to predictable changes in the global economy, you will find employment, economic stability, and preparedness for emergencies.

Protectionist threats from U.S. politicians, resulting from job losses to economies such as India and China, prompted U.S. Federal Reserve Chairman Alan Greenspan to offer a similar recommendation to the whiners. The only solution to foreign outsourcing of American jobs "is to boost the skills, and, thus, earning potential, of those lower on the skill ladder," he said in a speech to the Greater Omaha Chamber of Commerce. "These workers will need to be equipped with skills to compete effectively for the new jobs that our economy will create."

What does that mean for people who have lost a job or fear that they might? Go back to school, advises Greenspan. By doing so, skill-deficient employees can "address the apparent imbalance between the supply of such workers and the burgeoning demand for them."

Greenspan's comments were echoed in a report by City and Guild, the British vocational awarding body, which predicts that the key for a transient workforce in the twenty-first century is learning new skills. The study claims that U.K. workers starting from 2025 will have an average of nineteen different jobs during their working lifetime. One reason will be the growth of online learning that will allow people to retrain for new careers while in their current jobs. Other factors supporting the pattern are longer working lives because of greater life expectancy and uncertainties over pensions that will cause workers in their 60s to seek ways to supplement their retirement incomes.

"The trend for job and career diversity will grow considerably and employers can expect to see CVs landing on their desks from candidates who possess a broad range of skills," said Chris Humphries, the director general of City and Guilds. "This will inevitably mean companies start to judge potential employees on their transferable skills rather than just their sector experience. As a result, it will become increasingly important for individuals to extend their skills so that they can compete with other candidates."

### 6. The Advantages of Delayed Gratification

Mine is a frugal life. All I do is work, really—full-time during the standard workweek, and part-time on weekends. I don't go out drinking or partying. I don't shop for clothes more than twice a year. I rarely go to the movies or attend concerts. I don't have a wife or any dependents to support. Videos, books, CDs, good conversation, and exercise are my main forms of amusement, as well as the occasional dating.

The discovery that it's possible to live comfortably in Tokyo on less money than what popular opinion argues is liberating, indeed. Twelve hundred dollars a month is all that's necessary for my lifestyle here. Half covers my rent, utilities, and phone bills, thanks to living in a guesthouse with five other people. The other half is used for transportation, eating out, and entertainment. The monthly salary surplus stays in a savings account.

By sacrificing leisure and blind materialism, and by working three jobs, I paid off all of my college loans, tax bills, and debt. Then—and only then—did I start to enjoy life a little more. I moved into my own apartment in the suburbs of Tokyo, furnished the apartment, and splurged a bit on free time activities. Still, my cost of living is low. Most people increase expenses once they get a higher-paying job. That kind of behavior makes saving difficult because they are so busy trying to maintain an expensive lifestyle for others to see. I've already done that, and now prefer money in the bank over appearances of success. As my savings increased, I began to think about ways of securing a higher return than offered by the Japanese banks, which amounted to nearly zero percent.

Delayed gratification is difficult, but necessary to reach financial security. At the very least, money planners recommend aiming for an emergency fund of three to six months of living expenses. That will ease the pain of any sudden problems such as layoffs, illnesses, or family concerns.

### 7. The Merits of Tolerance
Suffer without complaining about the trivial, uncontrollable elements of life, such as crowded public transportation, long lines, and encounters with uncivilized people. The ability is not only needed for economic survival and a stable state of mind, but it also has health benefits.

A study published in "Circulation: Journal of the American Heart Association" examined the link between heart disease and psychological factors, irregular heartbeats, and risk of death in about 3,700 adults for ten years. The researchers discovered a significant connection between anger and hostility and health problems. Specifically, the analysis found that (1) quick-tempered men were more likely to die than those who stay calm; and (2) men who threw tantrums and were hostile to others had a higher risk of developing an irregular heartbeat, which can lead to sudden death from a stroke.

"There has been a perception that you can dissipate the negative health effects of anger out instead of bottling it up. But this was not the case in this study," said Dr. Elaine Eaker, president and lead researcher of Eaker Epidemiology Enterprises in Chili, Wisconsin.

## 8. The Disadvantages of Unemotional and Unintimate Sex

I have found that I'm physically stronger, more alert, and more productive each time I avoid unemotional sex. Failure to do so usually produces inaction, passiveness, late nights, late mornings, last-minute work preparation, and a total affliction of mental numbness.

The power of semen is one recurring theme in *The History of Celibacy*. "The urgency of conserving this vital fluid or 'life force' has led thinkers as disparate as Greek doctors, Hindu sages, athletics coaches, and moral reformers to proselytize for the celibate ideal with its promise that vigor, energy, and intellectuality will be retained along with the precious hoard of semen," wrote author Elizabeth Abbott, in her historical look at celibacy across three millennia. "French writer Honoré Balzac put it more succinctly when he groaned in postcoital tristesse, 'There goes another novel!'"

## 9. The Value of Monogamous Relationships

Freedom from the possibility of future pain and disappointment, irreclaimable time, and misplaced money comes with the decision to have just one partner at a time. Another equally important and obvious point is the much lower risk of contracting a sexually transmitted disease from such a union. In the age of AIDS, monogamy makes perfect sense.

Benjamin Franklin recognized the practical benefits of marriage. The inventor, businessman, philosopher, scientist, diplomat, and overall Renaissance man was a womanizer in his younger life, according to biographer H.W. Brands' book *The First American*. "That hard-to-be-governed passion of youth had hurried me frequently into intrigues with low women that fell in my way," Franklin once stated. But what became clearer for him was his preference for money over his carnal desires. Brand writes "money was tight and time tighter in the new business, and these liaisons 'were attended with some expense and great inconvenience'—not to mention 'a continual risk to my health by a distemper which of all things I dreaded, though by great good luck I escaped it.'"

## 10. The Stability of Our Origins

Self-transformation starts with the acceptance of our past without any shame or fear. Our history anchors the present.

## 11. The Power of Pep Talks

Whenever life reaches a low ebb, psyching oneself up with a private pep talk is an effective rallying technique. A few well-chosen words repeated inwardly or before a mirror, or read, have the ability to give you that much-needed boost to seize the day.

"Realize that if you want to accomplish in seven months what most folks don't do for their entire life, there will be sacrifices to make, folks who won't understand what and why you are doing what you are doing, sleep that will be missed, and you should feel uncomfortable as heck because you will and must do what you've never done before in order to harvest what you've never harvested before in such a short period of time," wrote Christopher M. Knight, a self-described wealth builder.

His sentence really got my juices flowing and pushed me into action. As a Japanese-language student at Middlebury College's summer intensive program, I experienced firsthand those words put into action. The beginner course crams a year of university-level Japanese into nine weeks of study. Just think, in thirty-six weeks, or nine months, one can learn the equivalent of four years' worth of college Japanese following Middlebury's system of radical study.

Another example of upbeat words that really did it for me was from Benjamin Franklin. In an excerpt from his autobiography, he wrote, "I have always thought that one man of tolerable abilities may work great changes, and accomplish great affairs among mankind, if he first forms a good plan, and, cutting off all amusements or other employments that would divert his attention, makes the execution of that plan his sole study and business...."

ဢ

My rehabilitation is nearly complete. I will never look down on a blue-collar worker, or any person making a living on a lower rung of the economic ladder. I will no longer take myself so seriously. I will never define myself by a company affiliation, a position, or an address. I will try to not allow other people's negative thoughts influence my actions. I will stop wasting kindness. I will save money. I will seek a relationship with God. I will find a suitable spouse and get married. I will enjoy life and live fully.

## A Note on the Type

The text of this book has been set in Goudy Old Style, one of the more than 100 typefaces designed by Frederic William Goudy (1865-1947). Produced in 1914, Goudy Old Style reflects the absorption of a generation of designers with things "ancient." Its smooth, even color combined with its generous curves and ample cut, marks it as one of Goudy's finest achievements.

Designed by Michael Dyer

www.ingramcontent.com/pod-product-compliance
Lightning Source LLC
LaVergne TN
LVHW011352080426
835511LV00005B/259